THE JEOPARDY! BOOK

THE JEOPARDY! BOOK

**The Answers, the Questions,
the Facts, and the Stories
of the Greatest Game Show
in History**

ALEX TREBEK

& PETER BARSOCCHINI

with an introduction by the show's creator,

MERV GRIFFIN

HarperPerennial
A Division of HarperCollinsPublishers

Jeopardy! and logo are registered trademarks of Jeopardy Productions, Inc.

FIRST EDITION

Library of Congress Cataloging-in-Publication Data

Trebek, Alex.
    The Jeopardy! book: the answers, the questions, the facts, and the
  stories of the greatest game show in history / Alex Trebek &
  Peter Barsocchini.—1st Perennial library ed.
      p. cm.
    ISBN 0-06-096511-8
    1. Jeopardy (Television program)   I. Barsocchini, Peter, 1952–
    II. Title.
PN1992.77.J363T74   1990
791.45′72—dc20   89-46490

90 91 92 93 94 CC/RRD 10 9 8 7 6 5 4 3 2 1

Contents

JEOPARDY THEME

Music by
MERV GRIFFIN

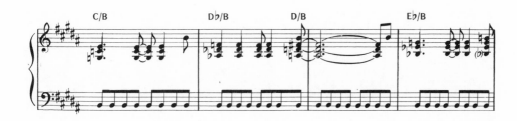

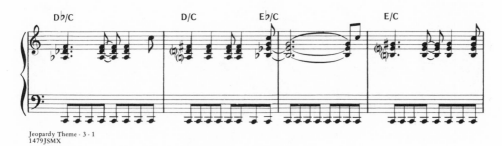

Jeopardy Theme - 3 - 1
1479JSMX

THE JEOPARDY! BOOK

Introduction

Merv Griffin

In 1962 I hosted my first talk show, a daytime talk-variety program that ran for six months on NBC then fell to the fate of cancellation; my success as a talk-show host was to come two years later. Despite the cancellation, the network was impressed enough to want to continue our relationship. I had hosted other shows for them, subbing for Jack Paar on *The Tonight Show, Play Your Hunch*—the highly rated daytime game show—and *Saturday Prom,* a show that somehow has escaped television historians. As part of my severance package for the talk-show cancellation, I negotiated commitments from the network allowing me to develop my own game shows; I was ready to sample the business from the other side of the camera.

I've always loved games. My family took long vacations when I was a youngster, during which my sister and I played Hangman in the back seat of the car. From Hangman, I later developed *Wheel of Fortune.* When I spent two years on the road with Freddy Martin's big band, crisscrossing the country in busses, I entertained myself with crossword puzzles. Even now my day begins with games: during breakfast I do the crossword puzzles from the *New York Times,* the *L.A. Times,* and *USA Today.* And last Christmas Dinah Shore enrolled me in a private crossword puzzle service that supplies me with new brain twisters every month.

So when I got the chance to develop my own games, I wanted to work with words and information. The problem was that after the quiz-show scandals of the late fifties, the networks were leery of shows where contestants answered questions for money. My wife, Julann, and I were discussing this subject on a plane flight in 1963. I mentioned how much I liked the old quiz shows, but reminded her that the scandals had created credibility problems for producers.

"So," Julann joked, "why not just give them the answers to start with?"

She was kidding, but the thought struck me between the eyes. She said to me, "79 Wistful Vista." And I replied, "What's Fibber McGee and Molly's address?"

I couldn't wait for the plane to land in New York so I could rush to the office and see if I could turn this little notion into a game. I decided to create separate categories of answers, such as History, Literature, Motion Pictures. Put the categories in columns and assign dollar values to each square. That was it. One big board with ten categories and ten answers in each category. We called the game *What's the Question?* and had a game board built to show to NBC.

Shows in development, such as the one I had in mind, are previewed for the network in run-through, similar to a play that's in rehearsal. We brought our *What's the Question?* to a small theater in Radio City Music Hall that could be rented for that purpose, only to find that our board took up most of the stage and protruded into the audience. There was barely enough space for the NBC executives to squeeze into the room.

Bob Aaron, then vice president of daytime programming for NBC, looked at our little run-through and was enthusiastic about the concept, but noted that the set was impossible to shoot. He suggested I reduce the game to specific rounds of increasing difficulty. NBC gave me the green light to develop the show further.

Using the dining room of my apartment on Central Park West as a run-through room, I called upon close friends and relatives to act as contestants, and set about the process of developing the answer-question format into a television show that today, if you will permit a moment of immodesty, is watched by more than fifteen million people every day.

The development process invariably involves trial and error, give and take, long days and late nights of brain storming; ideas are spun out, tried, twisted, sometimes kept, and more often discarded. I tinker, experiment, concoct, cajole, and try to remember that at the bottom of it all the game has to be fun not only for the people playing in the studio but, most important, for the viewers playing at home. As *What's the Question?* evolved, I created a first, second, and final round, now known as Jeopardy!, Double Jeopardy!, and Final Jeopardy! Since I'm a game player, I try to stick with my instinct about what parts of a game appeal to me; for example, I love horse racing, so I stirred into *Jeopardy!* the idea of a daily double. I had to fight the network to use the term *daily double* because they didn't like its gambling connotation. But I slipped it through, and it has become essential to the suspense of the game.

During the development process, I showed our efforts to network executive Ed Vane, who commented, "I like what I see, but the game needs more jeopardies." I didn't hear another word he said after that. All I could think of was the name: goodbye *What's the Question?,* hello *Jeopardy!*

After several more months of work I presented the revised game to the network for a final decision. We mounted a run-through for Mort Werner, then the head of NBC. The run-through was held in NBC's boardroom. I'd pasted flapless envelopes onto a large piece of poster board and filled them with index cards containing the answers. As I emceed, I lifted out the cards. Mort threw up his arms and complained, "I didn't get one right, it's too hard." As he said this, an assistant leaned over and whispered, "Buy it." The boss shook his head and said, "I think it's just too tough." And again, the assistant said, "Buy it." "All right," came the reply, "but it's on your head if it doesn't work."

That assistant was a young man named Grant Tinker, who, of course, went on to become a legendary production executive (of *The Mary Tyler Moore Show* and *Rhoda,* among others) and who, as president of NBC, is credited with taking that network from the cellar to the top of the ratings during the 1980s, championing such shows as *Hill Street Blues, St. Elsewhere,* and *Cosby.* His "Buy it" launched *Jeopardy!* onto the airwaves.

During its development phase, one aspect of *Jeopardy!* that appealed to the network was its humor, a fact that might surprise you since, even though Alex Trebek is a bright and witty man, *Jeopardy!* is not known as a hotbed of comedy. What happened in our early run-throughs was the answer-question reverse led to great fun. For example, if the answer was "Island that sold for twenty-four dollars," the contestant often came up with "Where is Manhattan?"; we'd ask for a rephrasing and get "How is Manhattan?" No. "Who is Manhattan?" It became funny, in the small office where we did the run-throughs, listening to contestants arm-wrestle the language trying to phrase the response in the form of a question. Since the networks were queasy about the quiz scandals, the idea of a humorous question-answer show appealed to them.

As soon as we put *Jeopardy!* on its legs, however, I realized it was unfair and boring to badger the contestant about being grammatically correct for every question. We were getting only twenty answers into a game, because the contestants spent their entire time trying to phrase the question correctly. We weren't ruling them wrong, we played with them until they got it right, but that idea went out the window. The show needed to be hard-edged and fast-paced if it was to endure, and it evolved in that direction.

In the early days of the show, as many of you will recall, we used terse, succinct answers—Answer: "Baja." Question: "What is lower California called?" All one- or two-word answers. But we ran short of the brief answers before long and had to start expanding. We added researchers to come up with challenging material for our very bright contestants. And then the NBC graphics department started complaining because our answers were getting wordier, hence more expensive to print on the cards. That became a running a battle with the network.

And the contestants caused some problems, too.

Our first contestant coordinator was a summer-stock director from Norfolk, Virginia, who had been an acting coach for my wife and for Gene Wilder. I figured if he could develop young acting talent, he would be able to spot good contestants. The problem was that he assumed all the smart people in New York lived in Greenwich Village, so in the first few months of the show a disproportionate number of contestants arrived with brooding expressions, dark capes swung over their shoulders, and books of poetry protruding from their pockets. People from the Midwest thought we were subsidizing every Marxist intellectual in the country. So we tried another contestant coordinator, and began to find contestants who were both smart and personable.

When it came time to choose our host, there was only Art Fleming. I saw Art in a TWA commercial, and he seemed authoritative, yet warm and interesting. Whatever product he was selling I was certain would be good. We called his agent, and although Art had never done game-show work, he was interested. He came in, tried out, and was the unanimous choice for host, a position he held for 2,858 shows. (You'll find an interview with Art later in this book.)

The show's announcer, Don Pardo, was a voice-over veteran I'd worked with on *The Price is Right.* I remember liking the urgency and excitement of his voice and thought him a perfect complement to Art.

Jeopardy! debuted on March 20, 1964, at 11:30 A.M. EST. Certain programmers told us we were in a death spot, because we faced reruns of the popular *Dick Van Dyke Show* at that hour, a show that even in reruns was considered to be invincible. But by the second or third week we were doing a 40 share (40 percent of the available audience was watching our show), and we didn't look back for the next eleven years. Within the first season, *Jeopardy!* moved to noon on the east coast, and that was a boon. It allowed people to watch the show on their lunch hours, and on college campuses all across America, *Jeopardy!* became noontime recreation. This created several generations of audience for us, many of whom are still with us, keeping the ratings of *Jeopardy!* high enough to qualify as the second-most-watched game show in history (right behind *Wheel of Fortune*).

The instant success of *Jeopardy!* shocked industry observers, since many felt the answers and questions were far too difficult for the average viewer. In fact, NBC research approached me shortly after the show went on the air and brought in charts and graphs that made a case for softening up the material; they contended that the material needed to be brought down to the level of the average thirteen-year-old, or we'd likely be off the air in a few months. I nodded agreement at this warning, then ignored it. In fact, I never even told the *Jeopardy!* staff about the meeting, because what appealed to me most about the show was its degree of difficulty. The question of the show's difficulty came up again in 1983 when King World, the current syndicators of the show, test marketed a new pilot version of *Jeopardy!* We were experiencing tremendous success running a nighttime version of *Wheel of Fortune,* and wanted to try *Jeopardy!* in the evening markets. But the research came back lousy, indicating that viewers weren't interested in *Jeopardy!* returning to television. Again, we ignored the research, thank goodness.

The show ran on NBC for eleven years, then was cancelled in 1975, not for bad ratings, but because, as networks sometimes do, NBC felt it was time to "redecorate" its daytime lineup of shows. That time period has never since duplicated the ratings strength of *Jeopardy!*—chalk it up to a bad roll of the dice. *Jeopardy!* came back to network television in 1978 for one year, then in 1984 reappeared in its current form, syndicated to two hundred stations across America and Canada. Foreign versions of the show play in seven countries. Ratings are higher than ever.

When the show returned in 1984, the search for a new host settled quickly on Alex Trebek. There was no intention to replace Art Fleming— it was just time to start a new tradition, and Alex rapidly established himself as the new "Mr. Jeopardy." So who better than Alex to take you on a behind-the-scenes tour of *Jeopardy!*—from game boards to statistics to stories about our wonderful contestants to facts about the mechanics of daily production.

Jeopardy! fans, here is your ultimate buffet.

The entire *Jeopardy!* family, from the show's producer, George Vosburgh, and his hard-working staff, to our syndicators at King World, to former associates, contributed to this volume. And we all have at least one thing in common with you: We love being in *Jeopardy!*

Warm-up
Jeopardy!

The name of this popular hodgepodge category is French for "rotten pot."

Including Final Jeopardy!, the number of categories on each show.

Heartthrobs, heavy metal, and very Grimm fairy tales were categories created for this tournament.

The same Honduras category appeared on *Jeopardy!* three times before any contestant did this.

So far we've only done one category about those darn people of ancient Etruria.

A letter or word in quotes in a Jeopardy! category means this.

In titles of categories this word has preceded cities, history, rulers, leaders, and trade.

Alliterative title for categories concerning alcoholic beverages.

The words *eke*, *nun*, *peep*, *kook*, and *kayak* have all appeared previously in this category.

The boss was our category about this man.

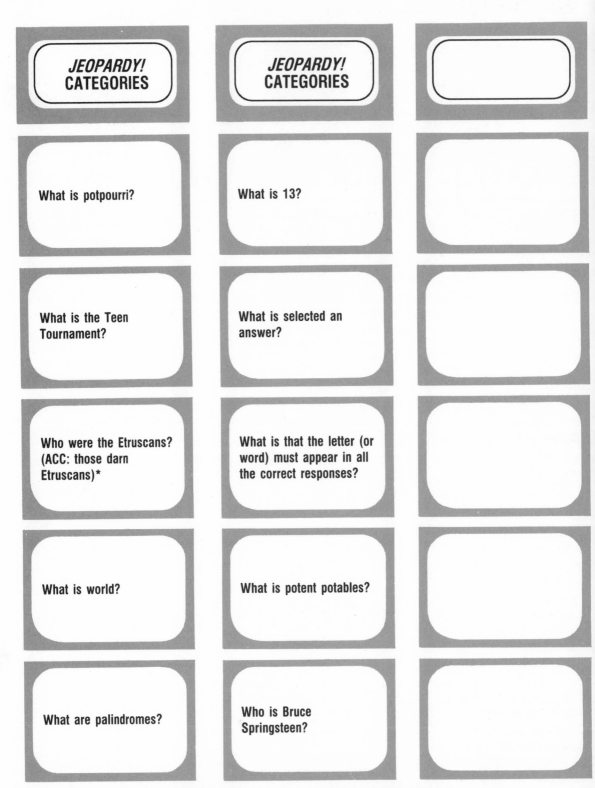

JEOPARDY! CATEGORIES	JEOPARDY! CATEGORIES	
What is potpourri?	What is 13?	
What is the Teen Tournament?	What is selected an answer?	
Who were the Etruscans? (ACC: those darn Etruscans)*	What is that the letter (or word) must appear in all the correct responses?	
What is world?	What is potent potables?	
What are palindromes?	Who is Bruce Springsteen?	

*"ACC" is a note written on Alex's game sheet instructing him to "accept" a listed alternative response.

A Word from Alex Trebek

My association with Merv Griffin Enterprises began, ironically, with *Wheel of Fortune.* Many years before the return of *Jeopardy!* to television in 1984, I received a phone call from *Wheel of Fortune*'s producer, Nancy Jones. At that time I was hosting another game show, but she asked if I would substitute for *Wheel*'s host, Chuck Woolery, who had suddenly become ill.

I taped several *Wheel of Fortune* shows, and returned to my other hosting duties. Then in 1983 I heard from Merv's company again. I was excited to learn that they were planning to bring back *Jeopardy!* and were interested in my hosting the pilot and series.

My formative years in broadcasting were spent with the Canadian Broadcasting Company, where I worked in national news, radio, and live coverage of special events. I had also hosted an information/trivia quiz show during the sixties. *Jeopardy!* seemed a natural step for me to take, with its unique blend of fascinating facts and information woven into an exciting game. Where else but on *Jeopardy!* can you win money by knowing that "the natural crystalline allotropic form of carbon" is a diamond, or be required to know "the last year in which the U.S. went for an entire calendar year without a vice president in office" (if 1964 comes to mind, then you might become a *Jeopardy!* contestant)? *Jeopardy!*'s combination of entertainment with education represents just the kind of programming I want to be involved with, and the invitation from Merv's company to participate in the show's resurrection was most welcome.

So in 1983 an updated pilot of *Jeopardy!* was produced. In television terms, a pilot is a sample episode of a program, produced as a showcase for network executives and station managers; the pilot becomes a prototype program that's also used to test market its appeal to sample groups of viewers.

When the *Jeopardy!* pilot was completed, however, we were not satisfied with the results. We were still using the old card-pulling system on the game board; somehow, as we raced into the high-tech eighties and faced the proliferation of video games and computer-generated imagery, this version of the show didn't feel contemporary enough, and the decision was made to further update the look of *Jeopardy!*

Jeopardy!'s game board was redesigned into a bank of video monitors, Merv rerecorded the famous theme music he'd written for the show many years ago, this time using the latest in electronic synthesizers, and the new *Jeopardy!* was readied for a fall 1984 launch. As we prepped the program for its return, it was my pleasure not only to host the show but also to produce it—Merv had definitely put my life in *Jeopardy!*

Our first year back on the air was a little shaky. Even though *Jeopardy!* had a tremendous cult following, many stations were uncertain whether America in the 1980s wanted to face such a challenging game show. During that initial season we aired at 2:00 A.M. in New York, and unless the viewers were insomniacs or irrepressible fans, they didn't know we existed. In Los Angeles we aired at 3:00 P.M. and were not pulling particularly good ratings. In fact, one afternoon I was being interviewed in my home by an important UPI correspondent, who admitted he hadn't seen the new version of the show, so I proudly flipped to our station, and instead of finding *Jeopardy!* was greeted by Jack Klugman in a re-run episode of *Quincy.* I called the station and was told *Jeopardy!* had just been cancelled. The fact that Quincy was a coroner seemed appropriate to me at that embarrassing moment.

Many stations thought our show was too tough, and buried us in difficult time slots. But we believed *Jeopardy!* was a show not simply for trivia experts, but rather a family program that viewers of various ages could enjoy, while measuring themselves against the television contestants. Merv has always created game shows that allow the home viewer to participate, and *Jeopardy!* is the perfect example of that philosophy.

King World persistently lobbied the marketplace for better stations and more advantageous time periods—and got them. The ABC station in New York bought *Jeopardy!* away from a competitor, and began airing the show in the early evening; suddenly we vaulted to the top of the ratings charts in this crucial market. The New York ratings turnaround was so stunning that eventually CBS moved the time of Dan Rather's news broadcast so that it would not compete with *Jeopardy!* Those ratings results caught the attention of station managers everywhere, and suddenly *Jeopardy!* began moving up in the national rankings.

The show that Merv Griffin developed in the dining room of his New York apartment soon became the second-most-watched show in the history of syndicated television (right behind another of his shows, *Wheel of Fortune*). Not only had veteran *Jeopardy!* fans returned to the show but a new generation of viewers discovered the answer-question format; the *Jeopardy!* "think" music was being played in baseball stadiums during pitching changes, college marching bands played it as part of half-time presentations; teachers were recommending that students watch the show during evening meal time, and were creating their own versions of the game to encourage student participation in class. "In the form of a question" had once again become a familiar American idiom.

Jeopardy! has always generated a lot of viewer mail: questions about the evolution of the show's format, inquiries about our categories and facts, postcards from former contestants who like staying in touch with the program, and requests from viewers for information about what has happened to some of our famous winners.

In this book we'll try to answer the questions we commonly hear about the show. We've asked champion contestants to share their opinions about strategy, and to tell us how they spent the prize money they won (one New York policeman decided to take his winnings and send himself to divinity school). The show's researchers will offer you clues about how they construct the answers and questions. *Jeopardy!*'s current producer, George Vosburgh, who initially worked on the show during its development phase in 1964, takes you on a tour of "A Day in the Life of *Jeopardy!*" And we've assembled an eclectic array of *Jeopardy!* game boards to challenge and entertain you. We have included some of our famous Tournament of Champions games, so that you can test yourself against *Jeopardy!*'s greatest players, and we've customized games so that you can really be challenged by certain of our best-known categories (how about Those Darn Etruscans for $1,000?).

For those of you who might even like to appear on the show, you'll find some sample contestant quizzes. You'll even find the sheet music to the show's theme!

And the best part of all—no commercials!

Onward.

American Shakespeare

JEOPARDY!

ANCIENT AMERICA	REVOLUTIONARY WAR	18TH-CENTURY AMERICA
The "Red Paint People" were paleolithic inhabitants of this state, now home of red lobsters.	Following his service in our revolution, Thaddeus Kosciusko led a revolution in this country.	In December 1783 General Washington resigned his commission before Congress in this Maryland capital.
Ten million years ago you couldn't get to the bottom of this 217-mile-long Arizona gorge; it didn't exist.	At the Battle of Bunker Hill, General Israel Putnam warned his troops, "don't fire until you see" these.	The first four of the Coercive or Intolerable Acts were passed in 1774 as punishment for this.
It was only ten thousand years ago that the last of these retreated over North America, leaving the now Great Lakes.	In February 1775 Parliament said this colony was in rebellion, thus allowing the shooting of rebels on sight.	The first census of the United States was held in this year.
All the encyclopedias used by *Jeopardy!* have the same painting of this ancient California cat, genus *Smilodon.*	On June 21, 1779, this nation declared war on Great Britain as an ally to the states.	In July 1701 this city had only one Cadillac— Antoine, its founder.
They were only connected from 26,000–8,000 B.C., which is why American human finds date back just twenty thousand years.	The Battle of Monmouth in this state was the last major battle of the Revolutionary War in the north.	Nickname of the man who said "First in war, first in peace, first in the hearts of his countrymen."

WAR OF 1812

After being burned in the war, the executive mansion was painted this color.

In 1813, Brigadier General William Henry Harrison recovered control of this Michigan city Hull lost in 1812.

The peace treaty to end the war was signed in the city of Ghent in this country.

President who, not knowing Britain had repealed the problem laws, asked Congress to declare war.

Two-word avian nickname given to Congressmen, like Clay and Calhoun, who favored battle.

CIVIL WAR

He commanded at the Second Bull Run and is said to have devised a sport that later used a bullpen.

As a nurse she treated Burnside's boys; as an author she wrote *Jo's Boys.*

In his 1862 inaugural address, Jefferson Davis noted the fact that it was this President's birthday.

If you saw a Civil War soldier wigwagging a commander in the field, he was doing this.

Head of intelligence under Gen. McClellan, after the war he went back to his detective agency.

19TH-CENTURY AMERICA

On April 30, 1812, the Territory of Orleans became this state.

In 1838, a Massachusetts law banned sales of this in quantities of less than fifteen gallons except for "medicinal purposes."

In 1816 this city replaced Chillicothe as capital of Ohio.

New York governor De Witt Clinton was considered the "father" of this massive project that opened October 26, 1825.

This man defeated Grover Cleveland in 1888 and lost to him in 1892.

JEOPARDY!

ANCIENT AMERICA

What is Maine?

What is the Grand Canyon?

What is a glacier?
(ACC: ice cap)

What is the saber-toothed tiger?

What are Siberia (Russia) and Alaska?
(ACC: Asia and North America)

REVOLUTIONARY WAR

What is Poland?

What are "the whites of their eyes"?

What is Massachusetts?

What is Spain?

What is New Jersey?

18TH-CENTURY AMERICA

What is Annapolis?

What was the Boston Tea Party?
(ACC: Massachusetts rebellious tendencies)

What is 1790?

What is Detroit?

What was "Light Horse Harry" (Lee)?

WAR OF 1812	CIVIL WAR	19TH-CENTURY AMERICA
What is white?	Who was Abner Doubleday?	What is Louisiana?
What is Detroit?	Who was Louisa May Alcott?	What is alcohol?
What is Belgium?	Who was George Washington?	What is Columbus?
Who was James Madison?	What is signaling him?	What is the Erie Canal?
What was "war hawks"?	Who was Allan Pinkerton?	Who was Benjamin Harrison?

DOUBLE JEOPARDY!

HAMLET

In one scene Hamlet tells her to go to a nunnery: In fact, he tells her five times.

He not only starred in the Oscar-winning 1948 film of *Hamlet,* he produced and directed it.

Hamlet speaks fondly of this jester while holding his skull.

Disparaging his mother's marriage, Hamlet says, "frailty, thy name is" this.

Claudius sends Hamlet to England with these two courtiers, but he escapes and returns to Denmark.

OTHELLO

Of Othello, Iago, or Desdemona, the character to whom Shakespeare gave the most lines.

Verdi's is "Moor" famous, but this *William Tell* composer wrote an "Otello" opera too.

This all-American football player scored in London as Othello in 1930.

Cassio calls this "an enemy" men put "in their mouths to steal away their brains."

Act I is set in Venice, but the rest of the play takes place on this Mediterranean island.

MACBETH

Of Lady Macbeth's 165 words in her sleepwalking scene, all but 20 have this number of syllables.

Peter O'Toole's Macbeth was called a cross between Vincent Price and this "Baby Jane" star.

The Queen Mother grew up there, Princess Margaret was born in it, and Macbeth was Thane of it.

"Macbeth" 's first performance was in this palace, once home to Henry VIII, which caught fire in 1986.

Because it's a bad-luck play, actors often avoid saying "Macbeth" using instead this geographical euphemism.

SHAKESPEAREAN OPERAS

This comedy was the basis for *Sir John in Love* and *Die Lustigen Weiber von Windsor*.

If you see *Puck, The Fairies,* or *The Fairy Queen,* you're watching operas based on this.

This play inspired the operas *La Furia Domata* and *Petruccio.*

Operas based on this comedy include *Hermione, Perdita* and *Ein Wintermaerchen.*

Two of three Verdi operas based on Shakespeare's plays, all with one-word titles.

MORE SHAKESPEAREAN OPERAS

Love story that was the source for this opera's "Tout Pour L'Amour" and "I Capuletti Ed I Montecchi."

Verdi's sleepwalking scene for this character is called one of the finest he ever wrote.

J. Paul Getty's son Gordon wrote a 1985 opera called *Plump Jack,* based on this comic character.

This comedy inspired Berlioz's 1862 opera *Beatrice et Benedict.*

This play begat at least two operas named *Viola* and two named *Malvolio.*

SHAKESPEAREAN ROYALTY

Hamlet was prince of Denmark, but Fortinbras was prince of this other Scandinavian country.

In *Troilus and Cressida,* Troilus's father is king of this.

At the start of the play named for him, this villain is the Duke of Gloucester.

Two of the three characters in *Macbeth* who were kings of Scotland both in the play and in history.

Play in which the King of Naples is shipwrecked by a sorcerer.

DOUBLE JEOPARDY!

HAMLET	OTHELLO	MACBETH
Who is Ophelia?	Who is Iago?	What is one?
Who is Laurence Olivier?	Who is (Gioacchino) Rossini?	Who is Bette Davis?
Who is Yorick?	Who is Paul Robeson?	What is Glamis?
What is "woman"?	What is wine? (ACC: liquor, alcohol)	What is Hampton Court?
Who are Rosencrantz and Guildenstern?	What is Cyprus?	What is "The Scottish Play"?

SHAKESPEAREAN OPERAS

What was *The Merry Wives of Windsor?*

What is *A Midsummer Night's Dream?*

What was *The Taming of the Shrew?*

What is *The Winter's Tale?*

What is *Otello, Macbeth,* or *Falstaff?*

MORE SHAKESPEAREAN OPERAS

What was *Romeo and Juliet?*

Who is Lady Macbeth?

Who was (Sir John) Falstaff?

What was *Much Ado About Nothing?*

What was *Twelfth Night?*

SHAKESPEAREAN ROYALTY

What is Norway?

What is Troy?

Who is Richard III?

Who are Macbeth, Duncan, and/or Malcolm?

What is *The Tempest?*

FINAL JEOPARDY!

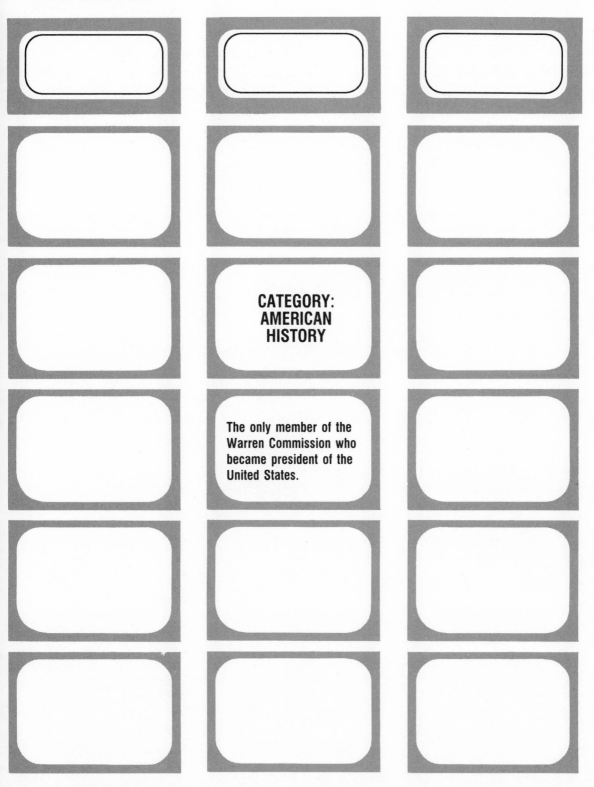

**CATEGORY:
AMERICAN
HISTORY**

The only member of the
Warren Commission who
became president of the
United States.

FINAL JEOPARDY!

Who is Gerald Ford?

Mondo Jeopardy!

JEOPARDY!

"M"ENAGERIE

As adults, these lepidoptera are harmless, but the caterpillars love to feast on your clothes.

Though its voice is shrill, this small monkey's name is derived from Old French *marmouser*, to murmur.

It's said ancient Romans not only ate these eels but fed their disobedient slaves to them.

Of the musk ox, musk deer, or musk turtle, the one that secretes the musk used in perfume.

These sled dogs were named for these Eskimos who, it's said, first bred them.

BEAUTY SECRETS

It's said eighteenth-century ladies wore special heavy nightcaps to keep these rodents from gnawing on their hairdos.

Pillows worn under gowns were all the rage when Marie Antoinette was in this condition.

Some French women used to paint these blood vessels blue to make them stand out.

Indian women supposedly used this bird's fat on their faces before the bird became our national symbol.

In *Caesar and Cleopatra*, Cleopatra tells the aging Caesar to rub rum on his head to make this happen.

STOCKINGS

Elizabeth I liked this country's hand-knit hose, but she defeated its armada anyway.

Even sea legs can look sexy enmeshed in these mesh stockings.

If you catch this bridal stocking accessory, it's said you'll soon catch a bride.

In the 1890s, women's everyday stockings were usually this color.

The title of a Betty Grable musical about vaudeville said *Mother wore . . .* these.

EDIBLE ANAGRAMS

Since olden days cooks have sprinkled this on food to make it last.

It comes from animals whether they're wild or tame.

You could eat this crustacean to bolster your courage—but it probably wouldn't help.

Pablo hid one of these in his coat.

Johnny is so cheap he put only one of these in the cobbler.

GUINNESS ANIMAL RECORDS

The largest one ever made by birds was built by bald eagles and weighed over 6,700 lbs.

A Texas cat named Dusty must have been the cat's meow because she had 420 of these.

Some of these arthropods have as many as 750 legs, not a thousand as their name implies.

The gaboon viper has the longest of any snake, nearly two inches.

It's the slowest-moving land mammal, and its name is a synonym for laziness.

DON'T MISS IT!

Tourists can shake hands with a dead crusader who's never decomposed in a crypt in this Irish capital.

The world's largest champagne glass bubbles away in this maestro's "wunnerful" museum.

Swan upping, the marking of the queen's swans, takes place on this London river once a year.

At a museum devoted to him, a wax replica of this 1930s criminal on the slab greets every "lady in red."

Evangelist Jim Bakker wanted to build a Golgotha theme park on the site where this occurred.

JEOPARDY!

"M"ENAGERIE	BEAUTY SECRETS	STOCKINGS
What are moths?	What are mice? (ACC: rats)	What was Spain?
What is a marmoset?	What is pregnant?	What are fishnets?
What are morays? (ACC: moray eels)	What were veins?	What is a garter?
What is the musk deer?	What was the eagle?	What was black?
What are malamutes?	What is to make hair grow?	What are tights?

EDIBLE ANAGRAMS	GUINNESS ANIMAL RECORDS	DON'T MISS IT!
What is salt?	What is a nest?	What is Dublin?
What is meat?	What are kittens?	Who is Lawrence Welk?
What is lobster?	What are millipedes? (DNA: centipedes)*	What is the Thames?
What is a taco?	What are fangs?	Who was John Dillinger?
What is a peach?	What is the sloth?	What was Christ's crucifixion?

*"DNA" means "Do not accept" the following answer.

DOUBLE JEOPARDY!

VERY GRIMM FAIRY TALES

When the miller's daughter guessed his name, he tore himself in two.

When "The Six Swans" turned back into boys, one boy still had one of these in place of an arm.

A severed one of these with a ring on it sealed the fate of "The Robber Bridegroom."

In "The Mouse, The Bird and The Sausage," this title character was swallowed by a dog.

At the end of the original version of "Cinderella," pigeons pecked out their eyes.

GOING IN STYLE

It's said the playwright Aeschylus died when an eagle dropped a tortoise on this.

This hirsute German movie star died in 1932, reportedly in Jean Harlow's arms.

"The Book of Lists" says a sixteenth-century man with the world's longest one of these tripped over it and died.

One of Henry Ford's most prized possessions was this inventor's dying breath, trapped in a bottle.

King who drowned himself and his physician in a lake near Munich in 1886, perhaps because he was "mad."

MUSICAL ANATOMY

Rudolph's red one was so bright it helped Santa guide his sleigh.

When these Irish organs "are smiling, sure they steal your heart away."

On "the good ship lollipop," if you eat too much—ooh! ooh! you'll awake with this kind of ache.

The Broadway song from *Wildcat* says, "Hey, look me over, lend me" one of these.

In *The Wizard of Oz*, the scarecrow sang about his desire to have this.

UNDERWEAR

It sells sexy lingerie and is a Hollywood Blvd. landmark.

They don't say Hanes until she says they say Hanes.

Of the story he designed her bra, Jane Russell said, "He could design planes, but a Mr. Playtex he wasn't."

You might be arrested if you wear only this undergarment while dancing to the waltz of the same name.

He cavorted as a leaf in a Fruit of the Loom commercial before his Oscar win for *Amadeus.*

MURDER AND MAYHEM

In this 1987 film, after one of the main characters was killed, the word "touchable" was written in his blood.

Some say he shot himself in Bolivia after soldiers killed Sundance.

Thousands of heretics were burned at the stake by order of this Catholic tribunal.

John Billington, who arrived on this boat, is generally considered America's first murderer.

These young killers were nicknamed "Babe" and "Dickie," as Clarence Darrow could have told you.

TABLOID TOPICS

A Soviet space probe discovered "ruined temples" on this fourth planet from the sun.

"The Ford Models," "Supermarket No-Cooking," and "Four-Day Wonder" are among tabloid versions of these.

A headline proclaimed "Bob Hope Owes Career Start to" this type of twins.

This raging mystery forest creature "Kills Two Scientists," says guide who survived.

The same week the *National Examiner* said antiperspirants cause itching, this paper said they relieve it.

DOUBLE JEOPARDY!

VERY GRIMM FAIRY TALES	GOING IN STYLE	MUSICAL ANATOMY
Who was Rumpelstiltskin?	What is his (bald) head?	What was his nose?
What was a wing?	Who was Rin Tin Tin?	What are eyes?
What is a finger? (ACC: a girl's finger) (DNA: a hand)	What was a beard?	What is a tummy ache?
Who was the sausage?	Who was Thomas Edison?	What is an ear?
Who were Cinderella's stepsisters? (DNA: stepmother)	Who was "Mad King Ludwig?" (ACC: Louis II of Bavaria)	What was a brain?

UNDERWEAR

What is Frederick's of Hollywood?

Who is Inspector Twelve?

Who was Howard Hughes?

What is a merry widow?

Who is F. Murray Abraham?

MURDER AND MAYHEM

What was *The Untouchables?*

Who was Butch Cassidy? (ACC: Robert Leroy Parker)

What was the Inquisition? (ACC: Spanish Inquisition)

What was the *Mayflower?*

Who were (Nathan) Leopold and (Richard) Loeb?

TABLOID TOPICS

What is Mars?

What are diets?

What are Siamese twins?

What is Bigfoot? (Sasquatch)

What is the *National Enquirer?*

FINAL JEOPARDY!

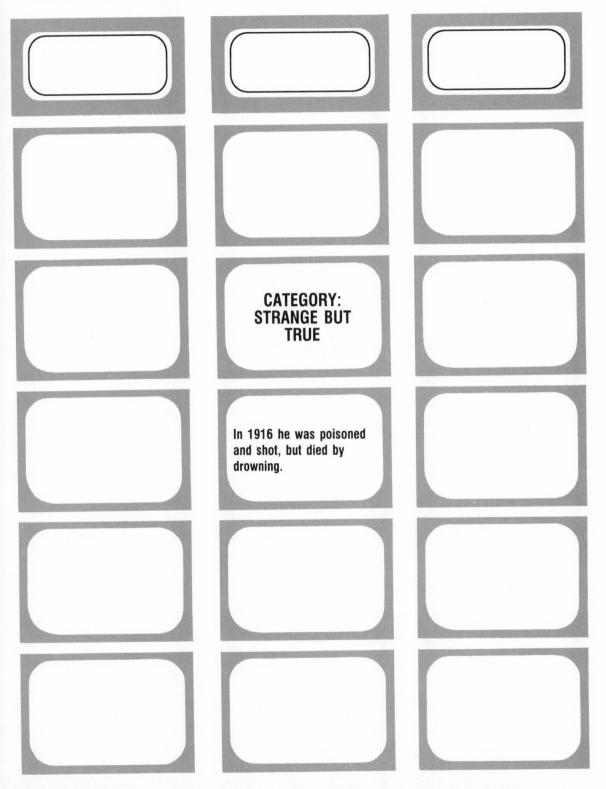

**CATEGORY:
STRANGE BUT
TRUE**

In 1916 he was poisoned and shot, but died by drowning.

FINAL JEOPARDY!

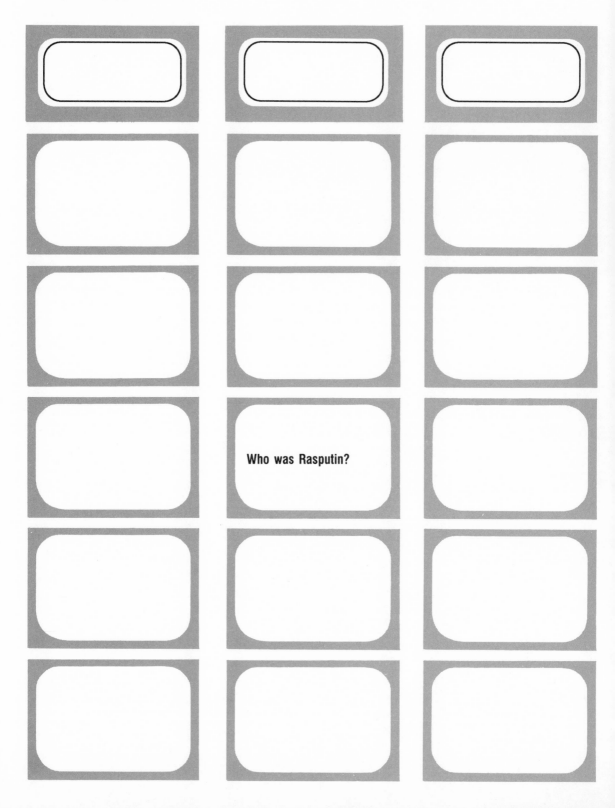

Who was Rasputin?

A Day in the
Life of *Jeopardy!*

George Vosburgh, Producer

The *Jeopardy!* production office and the studio in which we videotape the show stand on historic ground, at least by film community standards. Back in 1919, two of the fabled Warner Brothers moved from New York to Los Angeles to produce their own silent films. After renting space for a time, Sam and Jack Warner bought ten acres on Sunset Boulevard in the heart of Hollywood for a reported twenty-five thousand dollars.

The brothers built a production stage, offices for executives, producers, and writers, and a shop for scenery construction. At this new facility they cranked out their already successful serials and respected feature films such as *Beau Brummel* and *The Sea Beast,* both starring a young John Barrymore. In 1926 they embarked on their most ambitious project, one that would ensure the Warner Brothers' inclusion in Hollywood history books. The film was *The Jazz Singer* starring Al Jolson, the world's first "talking" picture. Portions of that film, including the synagogue scene, were shot on Stage Six of the rapidly expanding lot. In the 1930s, with talkies firmly established, the lot continued to produce hits. James Cagney mashed a grapefruit in Mae Clarke's face in *Public Enemy,* and Barrymore returned to star as the compelling *Svengali.* Subsequently, the studio changed ownership several times and, at this writing, Sam and Jack Warner's twenty-five-thousand-dollar investment occupies an entire city block worth somewhere in the neighborhood of a billion dollars.

Known locally as the KTLA Lot (for the call letters of the television station located there), the complex also contains a radio station, a technical operations center, office space, and nine sound stages.

Stage One, the northernmost in a row of five barnlike structures, is *Jeopardy!*'s dedicated studio. In television jargon "dedicated studio" means that the *Jeopardy!* set stands, whether or not we are taping shows, with none of the breakage, scratching, and scarring that occur each time the units are trucked from storage to the stage and back to storage again.

Diagonally opposite Stage One, across a narrow blacktop street that shimmers in summer and runs with a three-knot current in the rainy season, is the entrance to the *Jeopardy!* production office. Every business day, by 7:00 A.M. at the latest, the first staff member arrives, perhaps reflecting on the fact that he is walking in the footsteps of Barrymore and Jolson, or the pawprints of Rin Tin Tin, another early Warner star.

By 9:30 A.M., twenty-three people will have climbed the two flights of stairs (forty aerobic risers in all) and be at their desks in the third-floor office. The three members of the contestant staff will arrive later in the day, or, if they are on the road doing a contestant search, we may not see them for days.

Production of "the world's most popular answer-and-question game" moves at two distinct rhythms. The first is the steady pace of preparing shows to be taped. On those days, our researchers comb our extensive library of books and magazines, assembling the information that will end up on the game board. We handle ticket requests and organize the technical aspects of taping the show. The second rhythm kicks in on tape days; that's when everyone's tempo jumps to full throttle.

The staff is divided into three departments. In alphabetical order they are: the contestant staff headed by Susanne Thurber, the Production Department under Associate Producer Lisa Broffman, and the researchers who report to Editorial Associate Producer Harry Eisenberg.

As the name implies, the contestant staff is responsible for seeking out the extraordinary people who appear and compete on the show. In Los Angeles tests are conducted twice a day, at 10:30 A.M. and 2:00 P.M. At each session as many as seventy-five would-be contestants sit in the audience on Stage One, facing the *Jeopardy!* set, while they take the fifty-answer written test.

In an effort to prepare prospective contestants for actual show conditions, the test has been recorded on videotape. Each answer is displayed on a TV monitor accompanied by Alex Trebek's voice reading the answer, just as it would occur at a taping. After each answer, there is a pause for the contestants to write down their responses. Those who pass the written test play an informal version of the game, with tap bells to indicate "who pushed the button first."

On the road the procedure is the same although the locale might be a conference room or a hotel ballroom. On one college contestant search the setting was a tent on the seashore at Daytona Beach. In Belgium, England, West Germany, Italy, Japan, Korea, Okinawa, and the Philippines, under the auspices of the USO, hundreds of men and women in the United States Armed Forces have filed into mess halls and rec halls to take the *Jeopardy!* test.

The Production Department is responsible for everything involved in preparing and recording the shows for broadcast. Production is in charge of telephones, typewriters, and office supplies, taping schedules, crew calls, extra tech equipment, prizes and prize copy, coffee, bagels, donuts, and catering. These staff members look after a thousand details every day. Long before we enter the studio, one or another of the production assistants has painstakingly supervised the programming of each game on the Chyron. (A Chyron is an electronic device that stores the answers on a computer disk and pops them into our television monitors on demand.) After leaving the studio, one of the last jobs performed by production is shipping the completed shows to be closed-captioned for the hearing impaired.

The researchers are charged with authenticating every answer and question on the show. They make certain that the names are spelled correctly, that numerals within dates have not been transposed, and that the text displayed in our television monitors reflects accurately the facts set forth in the original reference sources. When each answer has been approved and edited to fit our space limitation of seven lines of text with fifteen characters per line, the categories are assembled into games and sent to the "round table."

Since roundtabling takes place at a long, rectangular table, the name signifies that, in the spirit of Arthurian legend, all participants are of equal rank and all opinions of equal import. One researcher reads the answers in a game and three or four others critique the material. By consensus answers that are insultingly easy, or impossibly difficult, are dumped and replaced.

Even though *Jeopardy!* is a syndicated show, since we air on two stations owned and operated by the Cap Cities/ABC Television Network, ABC is our "network of record." This means that we produce *Jeopardy!* under guidelines laid down by the ABC Department of Broadcast Standards and Practices.

ABC is not unique in having such a department; all three networks have similar units and their rules and regulations are basically identical. Among the many duties performed by the members of these departments is ensuring the integrity of the game shows that air on their respective networks. This is nothing new. When *Jeopardy!* first went on the air, in 1964, it was produced under the same strictures. These departments are in place to make sure that game rules are adhered to, that the games are honest, and that the entire enterprise is conducted in a fair fashion.

Years ago, I was producing a game show at one of the networks (not ABC) for the man (not Merv Griffin) who owned the show. We were in a network conference room, almost at the end of the second full day of discussions on security measures. I had not been in the business at the time of the quiz-show scandals so I assumed that this meeting was one conducted by men of mutually acknowledged probity—us against them. Then the discussion took this turn:

Owner: Let's give the winner of the game a lie-detector test after each show to see whether he or she has been given the answers. We don't have to test the losers because if they had been given the answers they would have won the game.

Network vice president: Sounds good to me . . . but, if we did that the ACLU would be all over us like a tent.

Owner: Who cares what that inconsequential bunch of radicals— hey, wait a minute. George is the only person on the staff who has access to all the game-show material. Let's give him a lie detector test after each show to see whether he has given anyone the answers.

Network vice president: Sounds good to me . . . no, there's only a fifteen-minute turnaround between shows. Lie-detector tests take a lot of time. It would extend the studio day and cost the network a ton of money.

Owner: Then let's sequester George in a motel, under guard. We can have his meals brought in. His wife can visit once in a while. We'll let him out every morning.

Network vice president: Sounds good to me. Nothing personal, George.

What happened to "us against them"? This was them against me! I was offended. They were discussing me in the third person and impugning my integrity in the bargain. After I calmed down, I realized that there had been nothing personal involved. The network VP was just doing his job. If anything dishonest did occur, he wanted to be able to testify in front of his bosses, the district attorney, the Federal Communications Commission, and the inevitable congressional investigative committee that he had taken all possible precautions to prevent it from happening.

As it turned out, I was not locked in a motel, but the show was produced under tight security, as is *Jeopardy!* Some of our security policies are covered in other parts of this book; here are a few more.

Contestant tests are conducted on the road, or on stage, in areas that are isolated from the offices in which answers and questions are prepared. There is no way that a prospective contestant could stray into the research spaces and observe or overhear an answer. Additionally, the contestant staff has no knowledge of the material contained in the categories or in the completed games.

While some of the researchers and some of the production assistants have knowledge of some of the completed games, no individual in research or production has knowledge of all the completed games. No one in production or research has access to the names and addresses of potential contestants.

Another safeguard is activated the morning of tape day. We submit eight complete games to ABC's Department of Broadcast Standards and Practices. From those eight, the ABC editor selects five games. This selection by an impartial third party determines not only the games that will be taped that day but also the order in which they will be taped.

At this time (9:00 A.M.) the names and occupations of the contestants are unknown to us. In fact, the contestant coordinators have not yet arrived at the studio, let alone the contestants themselves.

So, the next time you watch the show and there's a doctor, nurse, lawyer, or somebody from Cleveland in the game, don't be suspicious if one of the categories happens to be Medicine, Law, or Ohio. In a perfect world it would not happen that way. In the random selection of game material and contestants it does happen, but we certainly don't plan it that way.

After the ABC game selection (which we call "The Pick"), it gets very quiet in the office. Alex sits alone and goes over each game, underlining words that he intends to stress when he reads the answer and, occasionally, checking a fact, a spelling, or a pronunciation in a reference book. At around 10:30 A.M., Alex and I join five researchers at the round table and we go over the shows for the last time before taping.

This is our final opportunity to catch errors and update the game to keep pace with the rapidly changing world scene. For example, think back to late 1989 and early 1990 and remember the changes wrought by perestroika, the decline of communism and the fall of the Berlin wall, and the new heads of state in Haiti, Nicaragua, Panama, Poland, and Romania, among others.

While we are in the answer meeting, the thirty-three members of the stage, electric, and technical crew are busy with ESU (engineering setup) and our director, Dick Schneider, has arrived in his rental car. Dick flies in from New York before each tape session and returns on the red-eye immediately after.

Also at 10:30, the contestants are clustered at the gate, waiting to be escorted into the studio. The contestants will not be left alone, even to go to the rest room, until they have completed their competition or have been released to return to their hotel rooms and homes.

By noon, the answer meeting is over and Alex heads for his dressing room behind the audience on Stage One. For the next hour Alex can relax and return phone calls until it's time for makeup and to dress for the first show.

The contestants have received lengthy instructions from our staff, and security concerns have been covered by a representative from ABC Broadcast Standards. Now it's time for the rehearsal game in which each contestant takes a turn at selecting categories and amounts and, as much as possible, becomes comfortable with the buttons, microphones, lights, music, and sound effects of the game.

At 1:15 P.M. the audience files in and our announcer, Johnny Gilbert, starts his warm-up. He explains "television applause," the fast, staccato clapping that makes the 150 people in our audience sound like three times that number. He begs them not to blurt out any responses. On the rare occasion that someone in the audience does respond aloud we have to stop the tape to replace the answer and Alex hates to stop tape.

When it's time to start the first show, Johnny's warm-up is interrupted by a soft voice on the SA (studio address) saying, "Engineering, places. Cameramen, headsets, please." This is the TD (technical director) telling the crew to get into position and put on their earphones, so that he and the director can issue instructions during the show over the PL (private line). About a minute later the TD speaks again: "Tape is rolling."

Alex stands, just off camera, ready to make his entrance. The audience murmurs expectantly, and a globe girdled by the *Jeopardy!* logo swooshes onto the screen. Johnny Gilbert intones, "This is *Jeopardy!*" and the first show is off and running.

Jeopardy! is shot "live on tape," which means that while the show is recorded on videotape for broadcast at a later date it runs continuously in the studio just as if it were a live show. Barring a technical breakdown, an answer from the audience, or some other unforeseen problem, *Jeopardy!* clips along with only one planned tape stop. That is during the last commercial break just before Final *Jeopardy!* when the contestants are given pencils and papers to perform the addition and subtraction required to determine their wagers.

During the taping, our researchers listen to every response, encyclopedias at the ready, in the event that a contestant comes up with an answer we had not anticipated.

After the first show, Alex heads for his dressing room to change his suit, shirt, and tie. Usually Alex will not talk with the audience until he has one complete show under his belt. For the rest of the day, however, he will join Johnny Gilbert to tell stories and answer questions during each commercial break.

We tape three shows in a row with fifteen-minute turnarounds between shows and then take a meal break. Lunch is served on an adjacent sound stage by one of the five or six catering companies we employ just for variety. Each day we feed at least forty people counting our staff, the remaining contestants, guests, and a few members of the crew.

By 5:00 P.M. a new audience has been seated and will remain with us for the fourth and fifth shows of the day. After the final show, Alex will wave good-bye to the audience and thank them for their attention. Johnny Gilbert will hold the drawing for door prizes, and audience members, cast, company, and crew will head for home, while Associate Director Kevin McCarthy studies his notes for any small edits or "fixes" that must be made before the show is sent out into the world.

Tomorrow, we'll come back to the studio and begin the entire procedure over again, or we'll show up at the office to prepare shows for our next tape date. Either way it's a happy problem. *Jeopardy!* is an enormously successful show and we are all proud to be a part of it. I'm sure that no one will object if I take this opportunity to introduce the people who make *Jeopardy!* happen, just as their names appear on the crawl at the end of the show.

Executive Producer
MERV GRIFFIN

Produced by
GEORGE VOSBURGH

Directed by
DICK SCHNEIDER

Associate Producer
LISA BROFFMAN

Editorial Associate Producer
HARRY EISENBERG

Associate Director
KEVIN MCCARTHY

Stage Manager
JOHN LAUDERDALE

Assistant Producer
ROCKY SCHMIDT

Researchers
CAROL CAMPBELL
RUTH DEUTSCH
STEVEN DORFMAN
KATHY EASTERLING
DEBBIE HALPERN GRIFFIN
KIM GRUENENFELDER
CARLO PANNO
FREDERIK POHL IV
SUSANNE STONE
STEVE D. TAMERIUS

Art Director
BOB RANG

Production Coordinator
JOEL D. CHARAP

Material Supervisor
JULIEANN DAVIS

Production Assistants
KIMBERLY L. KOENEN
CAROLYN DONOVAN

Contestant Coordinator
SUSANNE THURBER

Co-Contestant Coordinators
GLENN KAGAN
KELLEY CARPENTER

Production Staff
CHRISTINA GABAIG
JUNE CURTIS
RON DAVIS
RENEE RIAL

Unit Manager
RAY REYNOLDS

Lighting Director
VINCENZO CILURZO
JAMES CARNE

Technical Director
RICK EDWARDS

Audio
JACK TOSSMAN
SUSAN BLUE

Camera
ROBERT FONAROW
RAIMO KAARTINEN
AL MILLER, JR.
JEFF SCHUSTER
MICHAEL TRIBBLE

Prop Masters
ROSCOE JOHNSON
COLE COONCE

Video
DICK BROWNING
ROSS ELLIOTT

Game Board Operator
DORIS DIAZ MONTES

Electronic Graphics
M. PATRICE LONG

Electronic Slide Storage
MICHELE HAMPTON

Videotape Editor
KIRK MORRI
JAIME FOWLER

Wardrobe
ALAN MILLS

Makeup
LARRY ABBOTT

Taped at
HOLLYWOOD CENTER
STUDIOS
Hollywood, California

Created by
Merv Griffin

Distributed by
King World

Celebrity Potpourri

JEOPARDY!

POTPOURRI	POET-POURRI	"PO"-POURRI
In 1987 the Hollywood sign was changed to read "Holywood" in honor of his visit.	Besides writing seafaring sagas, this New Yorker was a "whale" of a poet.	Its national anthem is "Jeszcze Polska nie Zginela."
It's been said this neutral country doesn't have an army, it is an army.	The Brownings spent most of their married life in this country and both of them died there.	Connemara, Dartmoor, Exmoor, or Shetland.
This fuzzy green fruit is also known as a Chinese gooseberry.	He wrote, "Oh, east is east, and west is west, and never the twain shall meet."	William Wordsworth accepted this honor on the understanding he would not have to write official verses.
Word acknowledging a witty remark that strikes home, or a hit in fencing.	Joyce Kilmer's most famous poem says, "only God can" do this.	Someone who steals a wild duck or cooks the duck's egg in boiling water.
In a nursery rhyme these body parts are described as "thirty white horses upon a red hill."	This popular American poet read his poem "The Gift Outright" at JFK's inauguration.	Chiropody.

POE-POURRI

Poe called it "this grim, ungainly, ghastly, gaunt and ominous bird of yore."

Poe joined this branch of the military under a pseudonym, Edgar A. Perry.

Young Edgar's foster family, they're reflected in his name.

The major East Coast cities in which Poe was born and died, they both begin with "B."

One of the three Poe stories in which the detective C. Auguste Dupin appears.

MORE POTPOURRI

Queen Anne's lace is the ancestor of this orange vegetable and has roots resembling it.

Its last line is "and crown thy good with brotherhood from sea to shining sea!"

This popular girl's name was originally the Celtic form of "Guinevere."

This publication says it's "no more a magazine about NYC than *Time* is a magazine about wristwatches."

Luxurious legwear, or a 1957 movie musical starring Fred Astaire, who didn't wear them.

STILL MORE POTPOURRI

A Cornell University survey found 66 percent of U.S. businessmen wear these too tight.

In Candlestick Park it's considered to be seat 24 in row 22 of section 61.

In Japan a man's is 9 feet × 1½ inches and a woman's, 12 feet × 10 inches; both wrap around kimonos.

In the seventeenth century Frederich William of Prussia banned peasants from doing this until they planted six trees.

To make these at home, heat carbon plasma to 20,000°C and condense it under ultrahigh pressure.

JEOPARDY!

POTPOURRI	POET-POURRI	"PO"-POURRI
Who was Pope John Paul II? (ACC: the Pope)	Who was Herman Melville?	What is Poland? (ACC: Polish People's Republic)
What is Switzerland?	What is Italy?	What are ponies? (ACC: ponies developed in the British Isles)
What is a kiwi? (ACC: kiwi berry, kiwi fruit)	Who was Rudyard Kipling?	What was Poet Laureate?
What is touché?	What is "make a tree"?	What is a poacher?
What are teeth (and gums)?	Who was Robert (Lee) Frost?	What is podiatry?

POE-POURRI	MORE POTPOURRI	STILL MORE POTPOURRI
What was "The Raven"?	What is the carrot?	What are their ties?
What was the (U.S.) Army?	What is (the last line of) "America the Beautiful"?	What is the worst seat in the house?
Who were the Allans?	What is Jennifer?	What is an obi?
What are Boston and Baltimore?	What is *The New Yorker?*	What is getting married?
What is "The Purloined Letter," "The Mystery of Marie Roget," or "The Murders in Rue Morgue"?	What are *Silk Stockings?*	What are (industrial) diamonds?

DOUBLE JEOPARDY!

CELEBRITY ODD JOBS

Singing bellboy Aaron Schwatt got this stage name from his hair color and the buttons on his uniform.

Picking cotton for ten years, she dreamed of singing with George Jones and later she married him.

He was a casket polisher, a swimsuit model, and a chorus boy in *South Pacific* before he played James Bond.

Once an elephant handler, he's now the world's best-selling western novelist.

A former circus fire-eater, he fired up critics with his acting in *Mona Lisa.*

CELEBRITY SECRETS

When this partner died in 1959, Bud Abbott was suing him for unpaid royalties.

Yoko Ono said it was these four who "broke up the Beatles."

While stranded on an island, this "Baby Doll" bit the head off a lizard and drank its "juice."

His ex-wife Anna Kashfi wrote that this *Sayonara* star made her dress like a geisha and wait on him.

In *Please Don't Shoot My Dog,* this child star said he was seventeen when Joan Crawford seduced him.

AKA

Born Raquel Tejada, she still uses her first husband's last name professionally.

It's Virginia Rowlands's stage name.

George O'Dowd's "juvenile" stage name.

This late French soprano, born Alice Josephine Pons, was married to conductor André Kostelanetz.

Karen Ziegler, whose films include *Easy Rider* and *Five Easy Pieces.*

Like Mary Pickford's, some of these Shirley Temple trademarks were stuck-on fakes.

She's no dummy, but her "brother" was, and Charlie's room was bigger than hers.

Late star who lamented "everyone wants to be Cary Grant. I want to be Cary Grant."

Shelley Winters said this *Bus Stop* star secretly lusted after Albert Einstein.

Number of Dale Evans's husbands before she rode off into the sunset with Roy Rogers.

Bobby Darin found out that the woman he thought was his sister was really this relative.

Heavy makeup and retouched photos hid this *Mildred Pierce* star's freckles from the world.

Sugar Babies star who said Louis B. Mayer's suicide attempt was her fault.

Her daughter revealed that Lena Horne went a few rounds romantically with this "Brown Bomber."

While under contract to Olivier, this *Network* star romanced Sir Larry's wife Viven Leigh.

He knew the honeymoon was over when Viven Leigh attacked him in his sleep.

This swashbuckler claimed in his *Wicked, Wicked* memoirs that he was once a slave trader.

Even his extramarital children didn't tear them apart; their mailbox said "Torn Page."

Afraid of being an "out-caste," this *Dark Angel* star passed her Indian mother off as her maid.

During WWI, a U.S. soldier "discovered" this hairy star on a battlefield and kept him in an oil drum.

DOUBLE JEOPARDY!

CELEBRITY ODD JOBS	CELEBRITY SECRETS	AKA
Who is Red Buttons?	Who was Lou Costello?	Who is Raquel Welch?
Who is Tammy Wynette?	Who are the Beatles?	What is Gena Rowlands?
Who is Sean Connery?	Who is Carroll Baker?	What is Boy George?
Who is Louis L'Amour?	Who is Marlon Brando?	Who was Lily Pons?
Who is Bob Hoskins?	Who is Jackie Cooper?	Who is Karen Black?

What are curls? (ACC: ringlets)	Who is Candice Bergen?	Who was Cary Grant?
Who is Marilyn Monroe?	What is two?	What was his mother?
Who is Joan Crawford?	Who is Ann Miller?	Who was Joe Louis?
Who is Peter Finch?	Who is Laurence Olivier?	Who is Errol Flynn?
Who are Rip Torn and Geraldine Page?	Who is Merle Oberon?	Who was Rin Tin Tin?

FINAL JEOPARDY!

CATEGORY: POTPOURRI

The last names of surveyors Charles and Jeremiah, who did their most famous work in the 1760s.

FINAL JEOPARDY!

Who were Mason and Dixon?

What Everyone Wants to Know

Do all the contestants get to keep the money they've earned?

Only the winner keeps the cash. The other contestants receive prizes. We get plenty of mail inquiring about this policy, since in the original version of the show, all contestants kept their earnings, regardless of whether they won the game. In the current version of the game show, money is basically a method of keeping score and translates to real dollars once you've won the show.

When the show was in preparation to return to the air in 1984, there was much discussion about this issue, and here are the reasons this change in the game was made. The sums of money a contestant can win on *Jeopardy!* are much greater now than in the original version of the show. For example, Burns Cameron, the Tournament of Champions winner in 1966, took home just over $11,000. Compare that to the $172,000 won by Chuck Forrest in 1984, and it becomes clear that we are dealing with a different sort of game. So we realized that in the new version of the show, three players could very easily reach Final Jeopardy! with five or six thousand dollars each. One or two of the contestants could look at the category, which might be Nuclear Physics, realize they have little knowledge in this area, and conclude that it will nice to go home with $5,000 in their pockets. They would wager nothing. In the older version of the show, with just a few hundred dollars involved, most contestants would take a whirl at it and risk it all with the hope of winning.

Even then, some were content to leave with small sums. "Some of the contestants were there just to pick up cash," recalls the show's first producer, Bob Rubin. "Once they built up a little money, they would protect it, wouldn't risk much, and didn't care if they came back on the show the next day. Others were only interested in winning, risked everything, and that made for the excitement. Women contestants were more apt to be protective of the money than men." There was one male contestant, however, who appeared on the show in 1967 with the express purpose of winning enough money to buy an engagement ring. He won a sufficient amount for the ring midway through the game and kept his mouth shut from there on. He did, by the way, purchase the ring, marry the girl, and remains married to her twenty-three years later.

But when the show returned in 1984, we knew that it was going to be sold largely for early evening time-slots, competing with reruns of sitcoms and, later, those tabloid shows; our product had to be exciting, and the key was a horse-race to the finish of Final Jeopardy! The other problem we anticipated was that if a contestant was running away with the show—$14,000 to, say, $5,000—the contestants with less money, knowing they cannot possibly win unless the leader made a historic blunder, would not even participate. So by changing the rule to allowing only the winner to keep the cash (although there are occasions when someone is so far ahead Final Jeopardy! has no suspense) more often than not the outcome of the game remains undecided until the final seconds.

We feel this rule change put even more jeopardy into *Jeopardy!*

In the original version of the show, contestants were allowed to ring in as soon as the answer was exposed, but not now. Why?

That is the other major difference in today's *Jeopardy!* and, again, it has to do with the evolution of the game, rather than random tinkering with a winning format. In the original show, contestants were permitted to ring in the moment the answer was exposed; they did not have to wait for Art Fleming to finish reading it. Now remember, in those days the game board consisted of printed cards that were manually exposed by stagehands. "In some cases," notes Bob Reuben, "contestants rang in on reflex, and we'd get that horrible blank look on their faces when they realized they'd pressed in too soon. We helped combat that by varying the pulling of the cards. So when Art said, 'The answer is,' which was their cue to pull, the stagehands were instructed to sometimes take two beats, one beat, pull immediately, so that if a contestant was anticipating the pull, we'd clear the light on their podium. In this manner we tried to prevent one incredibly fast person from dominating the game. Of course, since this was a hands-on manual operation, sometimes the cards got stuck and the contestants looked like racehorses trying to bust out of a stuck starting gate.

"This also affected the way we structured the answers. For instance," Bob continues, "as the show evolved, the games became more sophisticated. If the category was Explorers, the contestant picked the $10 window, and the answer was 'He discovered America,' then obviously the correct question was Columbus, no tricks involved. But in the $100 window, no way was the correct question going to be Columbus; there'd be something else in the structure of the answer that led to Vespucci, Lief Ericsson, or the like. Every word counted and we learned to bury the key clue at the end, so contestants wouldn't be constantly jumping in. 'Nixon ran for this office in 1962'—if the contestant rang in on Nixon and the 2 at the end of the year wasn't exposed, they'd miss it."

The 1984 *Jeopardy!* debuted with this rule intact, but by then we were using an electronic game board rather than stagehands. Contestants could still ring in the moment the clue was exposed. And this began causing no end of problems. Once a contestant selected a category and dollar amount, Dick Schneider, our director, would cut to a shot of the clue, and stay on it until I finished reading the answer. Invariably, a contestant would ring in while I was still reading.

First, the sound was distracting to the viewers. We started getting complaints from viewers and stations that the buzzing was irritating them. Second, once a contestant rings in, a five-second timer is activated. Often, contestants rang in so quickly that by the time I finished reading the entire clue, their five seconds had expired, and another contestant had rung in. Sound confusing? If so, you're not alone. Viewers were baffled that I wasn't allowing the first person to ring an attempt to supply the correct question, but we couldn't stop the show to explain that their time had expired. Also, certain contestants were so bright in the first *Jeopardy!* round—where the material is slightly easier than in Double Jeopardy! or Final Jeopardy!—that they wouldn't care what the category or dollar amount was, they simply pressed in immediately, realizing that by the time I'd finished reading the clue, they would in all likelihood come up with the correct question.

One day we had a contestant who continually pressed the buzzer with such fervor and physicality that not only did he ring in first everytime but his opponents were so distracted by his gyrations that they basically threw in the towel. Consequently, we decided to install a lockout device that requires a few tenths of a second in between depressions of the buzzer for the system to reset itself; if you constantly jiggle it, or keep it permanently despressed, you will never complete the current necessary for ringing in. This prevents one contestant from dominating the system.

Then the following season we further changed the rules to allow contestants to ring in only when I finished reading the clue, rather than upon its exposure. We had to make this change because constant ringing had become such an irritant to the home viewer. Some *Jeopardy!* fans argue that this change altered a basic tenet of the strategy, but one has to realize that we are producing a television show, not simply an in-studio quiz for contestants. It is vital that the home viewer participates in the program, or there is no program. Now we cut away from the game board just before I finish reading the clue, so the home viewers can view the three contestants, see who rings in first, and gauge their own speed against that of the people playing in the studio.

Again, this choice was made for home involvement, not entertainment reasons, because *Jeopardy!* is sold in syndication on an individual basis to stations throughout America, making us more susceptible to audience taste than was the case with the original show. When *Jeopardy!* played on the NBC network, if the show did well in St. Louis, but not particularly well in Chicago, that did not mean the Chicago station would drop the show—it was part of the network. In syndication, if a particular station doesn't like your show it will dump it faster than yesterday's fish. We simply felt the integrity of the game was not compromised by the change, and the stations and viewers have responded favorably. We still structure answers, in most cases, so that players have to hear or read the entire clue to respond correctly. Of course, remember that many of today's contestants have been watching the show for twenty years, and are familiar with the way we do things, so they successfully anticipate where a clue is leading, buzzer or no buzzer. We actually get a better game by eliminating the pure reflex speed as a determining factor.

Some contestants seem to have an easier time ringing than others . . . Why?

When you watch the show frequently, you'll see contestants who are unable to signal for long periods of time, even though it appears they may be trying to; then all of a sudden they get the hang of it and start signaling first and controlling the board, and I know people wonder how this is possible. My observation is that contestants come upon categories that boost their confidence, relax and focus them, make them feel positive about their abilities and their potential to win the game. When you feel that way, your reflexes work more efficiently. I'm sure you've had the experience of being in a stressful situation, and somehow you can't get your mouth to form the words you want, but later on you think of all kinds of clever things you should have said. That's *Jeopardy!* If a player hesitates for a moment, feels apprehensive about signaling, then that one one-hundredth of a second might be all the time it takes for an opponent to beat him to the punch.

I've also noticed that contestants who are trailing often have trouble signaling, and that's because they are being tentative, they're thinking, "Geez, she's three thousand dollars ahead of me. If I ring in now on this thousand-dollar clue and miss it while she gets it, I'll be down five thousand dollars." I see this process flash across their eyes in half a second, and suddenly they can't signal to save their lives. Usually it has to do with the categories. We reveal the board and a particular contestant knows everything about Civil War and Classical Music, but the categories up there are English Lit, Malaysia, Geography, Food Facts, Sports, and Movies. And I see the cloud of anxiety settle over the contestant. In the next round, sure enough, up come Civil War and Music, and that same contestant lights up and rings in with ease.

I've seen over two thousand contestants on *Jeopardy!* and I witness this scenario on a daily basis. Signaling is all about confidence. When I was producer of the show, and briefed the contestants before taping, I told them that they, based on their tests, were probably all equal in terms of knowledge. But what we never know until the lights go on and the music plays is how well someone is going to deal with competition and adversity. Some people are very smart, but timid, and those people have a hard time winning on *Jeopardy!*

Many former champions report being completely unaware of their monetary standing during the rounds. They just played, and checked the money at commercials, when they can take a deep breath and sort things out. If they try to follow their standings as they play, it impairs their ability to respond. As one former champion put it, "I was so into the game, having such a good time, I was always surprised how quickly the commercials rolled around. And when I looked at the totals I was shocked at how far ahead I was. I really had no idea. I was just playing the game and having a good time."

Do you offer contestants any advice before the show?

Let me begin by telling you one of the secrets to winning. Maybe I shouldn't say *secret* since we share it with everyone who comes to the studio. There is a briefing prior to taping when we share with the contestants what we know about playing the game; most of the big winners are able to put what we say into practice, while certain contestants cannot, only because of the pressure of the situation. When I used to do the briefing, during the first few seasons, I told the contestants, "Look, you're playing with house money, you can't lose a penny of your life savings here. You're not going to solve the world's famine problems here, you're not going to make an impact on the world political scene. This is not glasnost. This is a half-hour television quiz show in which you get an opportunity to enjoy twice the length of time that Andy Warhol said everybody would be famous for by the year 2000.

"Your friends, relatives, and acquaintances will get a chance to see you on television. So why not enjoy the moment for what it is, look upon it as fun, rather than a moment that is going to change the course of your life? Yes, you can win some money on the show. But you'll still be you when you walk out of the studio. The people who love you when you walk in here will still love you when you walk out, and the others you shouldn't be too worried about, anyway. And if you don't win, just consider the fact that on a different day, with different categories on the board, you might well have been the champ."

One of the keys to this is that when people realize they are going to be on national television, they become more concerned with not making fools of themselves than with actually playing the game. The ego gets in the way. And that happens to a lot of people. Not wanting to fail prevents them from succeeding. For most contestants, worrying about this summons a tension level that impairs their reflexes. Sure, some people do better when they're edgy. But most don't. That's one of the primary reasons we have that little break in the first round when I talk to the contestants.

We start the game, let them get the feel of being on camera and performing under pressure, then we go to commercial and come back for a chat. What contestants experience is that the game moves so quickly, shockingly so, that if they're bundles of nerves, the whole thing is over before they come out of the fog. So we take that early break. During the commercial, our contestant coordinators come on stage to talk to the players, encourage them, or tell them that they're anticipating the buzzer. Then I'll step over and talk with them about something that has nothing to do with playing the game, just something to take their minds off the pressure of the moment. They can take a deep breath.

We come out of commercial and I speak with them on camera and, again, it gives them the opportunity to settle in. Whereas if we didn't break there and just pushed through the first round, many players might get so caught up in a negative rhythm of ringing in too soon, or freeze under the lights, that the round would be over before they ever had the chance to participate. You'll notice in big sports events that if a team gets off to a weak start, the coach will often take a quick time-out to settle his players. It's the same here.

To do well on *Jeopardy!* contestants must remember they're playing a game, and treat it as such.

What characteristics do good Jeopardy! contestants share?

I think we basically see two groups of people. First, the professional people, lawyers, teachers, State Department attachés, people who make a living by having vast general knowledge, and the ability to summon it quickly. Then there are the people who are trivia sponges, readers who soak in literature and history and popular culture, and for one reason or another, retain it all. It's a knack, a gift, more than a skill. There are plenty of brilliant people walking around who would do poorly at *Jeopardy!* because of the time constraints. Certain people do wonderfully on the written contestant test, but when they play the mock game with our staff, their brilliance goes south. It's not about how much you know, it's about how much you know instantly. All *Jeopardy!* winners are big readers, that's certain, and most of them want to appear on our show only. They're not interested in dressing up like a banana and picking what's behind a door. Usually, they've watched the show for years and have the itch to give it a try. Again, though, one common characteristic of the winners is that they show up to have fun. They don't turn it into life and death, and don't judge their self-worth by how much they win on our show.

Do you think someone can actually prepare to be on the show?

Basically, you either know the stuff or you don't. It's a good idea to refresh knowledge in certain categories. Americana, Presidents, Movies, the stuff that comes up a lot. But much of our material is drawn from what's happening currently in the world; newspapers and magazines are a good source of general information about current events. You had better know Shakespeare, because if you have trouble remembering whether he wrote *Antony and Cleopatra* or *Caesar and Cleopatra,* then you may run into problems on the show. All you can do, really, is enhance what you already know. Some people bury themselves in trivia books and almanacs, but my suspicion is that they aren't the ones going home with the big bucks. If you haven't got it, you're not going to discover it a few days before the show, but in that case you've probably been weeded out during the selection process, anyway.

Yes, there are contestants who bury themselves in trivia books the night before taping, and a question comes up relating to something they've just read. But more often than that, contestants who overload on preparation will short-circuit when the time comes to play the game.

What about mistakes on the show . . . how often do they happen?

Not often. *Jeopardy!*'s original producer, Bob Rubin, recalls that "we made about four mistakes a year, and if they affected the outcome of the game, we'd bring the contestant back, of course. Often, the mistakes came from books that made mistakes. That happens. We used to get a lot of mail claiming more mistakes than we actually made, even about the names of categories as innocuous as Potpourri (a *Jeopardy!* favorite). For instance, I received one particularly irate letter from a gentleman who wrote that he was 'sick and tired of Catholics dominating America, and that it was an affront to people of other religions that we devoted an entire category every week to Catholic information.' As the letter went on I became more and more confused, until he summed it all up by saying, 'How dare you have a category called 'Popery.' "

To this I say amen because we do make mistakes on the show, but not nearly as many as viewers accuse us of. Usually, the viewer will not hear the entire clue, and fire a missive off to us about the part he did hear.

A few years back we did a Final Jeopardy! that elicited an avalanche of mail. The answer was 'The last president to appoint a Chief Justice of the Supreme Court.' The correct response was 'Who is Nixon?' for appointing Warren Berger. Well, one angry batch of letters arrived accusing us of being antifeminist; they felt the correct response was Sandra Day O'Connor, appointed by Ronald Reagan. Another batch lashed out at us for hating Ronald Reagan, since he appointed O'Connor, and we had chosen to ignore this fact. I wrote back to these people reminding them that they had missed an essential clue: *Chief* Justice. Many of our "mistakes" fall into that category.

Jeopardy! is held to a standard second only to that of the Librarian of Congress. And mistakes do happen. During the 1960s I did a teen quiz show in Canada where the material was prepared and carefully checked. Then it was sent to a teacher for proofing. Then to the show's judge, a former deputy minister of education for the Province of Ontario, and he checked it. Then we gave it a final check before airtime. Still, we made mistakes.

Sometimes we'll have a medical question and have a doctor for a contestant, and though our medical question came out of a text, he's got ten years of specialized study in the area and he'll pop up with three alternative answers to ours. Perfection is not possible.

I did calculations on our mistakes during the 1984, '85, and '86 seasons, and learned that our accuracy rate was 99.5 percent. Hey, Ivory Snow is only 99.44 percent pure, so my conclusion is that our batting average is damn good.

Did you have any second thoughts about hosting a show that had come to be so identified with Art Fleming?

Art was an excellent host for the show, so all I could do was take my own approach, be myself, and let the viewers decide how they felt about it. That's the way the entertainment business is. In my first year I received maybe a dozen letters comparing me to Art, people writing to say that nobody will ever match Art Fleming on *Jeopardy!* Art was terrific, I try to do a good job, so I leave it at that. But there was one woman who wrote a particularly vehement letter just a few weeks into the new version of the show, suggesting I drop off the face of the earth because only Art can host *Jeopardy!* So I wrote her back and told her that I can understand why she'd be a big fan of Art's. I used to watch him, too. But I pointed out to her that she had ten years to get used to Art and to know him, and that she'd only given me two weeks. To her credit, she wrote back a nice letter in which she promised to give me a longer tryout and, in fact, she had continued to watch the show after writing her first letter and was actually enjoying it. So that pleased me.

How did the different tournaments come about?

The original show had its Tournament of Champions, and over the years we've added the Teen Tournament, Seniors Tournament, and College Tournament, and they've all proved to be very popular. People love watching the kids play, to see how many bright young people are out there. We constantly read about the problem kids in society, so it's nice to see the flip side of this on *Jeopardy!* We get tremendous ratings for the Teens.

The Seniors Tournament is a story in itself. In 1986 I realized that in my three years of hosting the show I'd only seen one contestant over sixty actually win a game. This bothered us on two levels. People past the age of fifty do not lose their intelligence, and we knew there was a huge audience out there who wanted to root for someone their own age, someone they could identify with. The reason so-called senior citizens were not winning on *Jeopardy!* was simple: reflexes. Playing *Jeopardy!* not only requires knowing the information, but also the ability to signal with tremendous speed. When we get older, we slow up. Just as pro athletes lose a step later in their careers, it takes us an extra beat to think and react to answers and questions as the years roll on. So we decided to try a Seniors Tournament, open to anyone over the age of fifty.

Well, I started getting letters from angry viewers saying "How dare you refer to people over fifty as seniors?" My response is that *senior* is a relative term. Pro basketball players are senior by age thirty, so are hockey players. Pro golfers generally lose their putting touch somewhere in their mid-forties and count the days until they hit the senior tour at age fifty. In *Jeopardy!* a good thirty-year-old contestant will beat a good fifty-year-old contestant every time. The neurons fire faster, and the reaction time is better. So we gave our seniors their own tournament, and viewers of all ages watch it. And just as adults like to see kids do well, we've found that kids like to see the older generation do well. For example, Ouida Rellstab, a Senior Champion from Louisiana, became quite a celebrity after winning on *Jeopardy!* She teaches ninth-grade English at a private school near New Orleans, and whenever she makes an appearance in the hallway, she can hear strains of the *Jeopardy!* theme being hummed all around her; and when she asks a student a question in class, the other students pipe in with our "Think" music from Final Jeopardy!

One of my favorite exchanges with a contestant took place with the Senior Champion Peggy Kennedy of Flushing, New York, who works as a forensic toxicoligist.

Alex: We introduced you as a forensic toxicologist.
Peggy: That's right.
Alex: Which means you do what, precisely?
Peggy: I analyze body organs, tissues, and fluids for drugs and poisons for the New York State Police.
Alex: I see. I've got to be dead before you get to analyze me.
Peggy: That's right. I'm sorry, we won't have anything to do with you when you're alive.
Alex: You're not the first woman to have said that, believe me!

All of the Tournament of Champions winners have been male . . . any comment?

Most of the contestants are male, for starters. The percentage of men trying out for the show is higher, about 70 percent male to 30 percent female. It wasn't always this way. In the 1960s there were always more women applying to the show, by almost two to one. Of course, in those days, the show aired in the mornings, and the audience was predominantly female, so that might have been a contributing factor. But today it's mostly men who try out, though the percentage of female applicants increases when we do contestant searches outside of Los Angeles. The percentage of men and women passing the contestant quiz is the same, but the winners tend to be male.

As to actual contestants who make it to the show, we try to even things out by including enough women to make it about sixty-forty male-female. Obviously, we have to test many more women to fill our pool than men.

Bob Rubin contends that from the first day of the show, men were the go-for-broke players. They would risk more money and play the game more aggressively than female contestants. Susanne Thurber, our contestant coordinator, reports that during the tryouts men continue to be the aggressors, that some women are less inclined to attack the board than men are. The press has quizzed me on this matter frequently, and I believe that the answer lies in the competitive environments in which males have grown up. Our baby boomers, who make up the majority of our contestants, grew up in a society where boys still wanted to run faster, throw a ball farther, and be able to name the National League batting champions for twenty seasons. Men today are still fascinated by useless statistics, the kind that jam the sports sections of the newspaper. So when you've got a game that involves summoning mounds of trivial facts, it's going to attract more men than women. Today's children are being reared differently, and so we'll probably see a gradual evening out of the male-female win ratio on *Jeopardy!*

What we do find on *Jeopardy!* is that when female contestants surface who have the same kind of trivia interests as the males, and who like the aggressive game, they do equally well. It's just that for every seventy male contestants who fit that category, we can find only thirty females.

I've noticed a difference between men and women in wagering, as well. Women tend toward the conservative when hitting a Daily Double, or entering the Final Jeopardy! round. Men tend toward the go-for-broke attitude, and this helps their winning percentage.

We cannot control the outcome of the game, but we do try to present a balance of categories that would not favor any certain type of player, male or female.

How does someone qualify to be included in the Tournament of Champions?

The tournament consists of all five-time winners from the regular season, the winners of the Teen, Seniors, and College tournaments, plus the highest-scoring four-time winners. A total of fifteen players make it to the tournament each year.

How are the categories chosen?

By the producer of the show, George Vosburgh. Generally we'll balance the board by blending "serious" categories like Geography and History with lighter stuff, Movies and the like. Double Jeopardy! will tend toward the serious. When it comes time for the Tournaments, we choose our categories and then the researchers prepare special games to fit the occasion.

What about strategy?

There are many different approaches, as you'll read about in the contestant section of this book. The contestant everyone still remembers from the new version of the game is Chuck Forrest, the 1985 Tournament of Champions winner. He was so good that he basically intimidated the other contestants in the tournament; you could hear them backstage talking about who might take second place, because they just about assumed Chuck would win it all. Right there is a piece of advice: You have to go in expecting and wanting to win it all, because if you don't, you'll play the game too conservatively and not give yourself a chance to win. But aggressive doesn't mean reckless.

Chuck advises other contestants not to guess, to ring in only when you're fairly certain of your ground. This is solid advice, unless you are far behind, running out of time, and need to go for broke. One of Chuck Forrest's winning strategies was to jump around the board so that other contestants couldn't get their heads locked into a category and get comfortable with it. He was like a pitcher with a great repertoire; he kept the other contestants off-balance. This strategy, however, wouldn't work as well today. As the years have gone on, the contestants have become even more versatile in the areas of their knowledge, and I have seen several who might have kept up with Chuck's scattershot approach.

Some contestants like to start at the bottom of the board, to rack up the big dollars right away. I advise against that. If you start at the bottom, you don't really have a feel for the category; there may be a flow and a style to the answers that will be evident if you start at the top with an easier clue. I have seen many contestants think they'll throw everyone off by cleaning out the big-money windows, only to put themselves in very bad positions. We construct the board to help lead you into the more difficult clues, and since in most games we end up covering the entire board, you'll have your chance at the expensive clues, so why not let yourself settle in before tackling them?

In the first round, my advice to players is to be aggressive, try to get a rhythm going, build confidence. If you hang back, the confidence factor might shift to an opponent, and even if that opponent might not be as good an overall player as you, the confidence of a solid first round might change the balance of power. In the second round, you can become more strategy-conscious, more judicious. We've got big money on the board in this round, and two Daily Doubles; this is where you need to be smart, where you don't want to take foolish chances you might have gotten away with in the first round. But when the opportunity to go for it presents itself, then go for it you must. For example, if you are in a category you're comfortable with and you hit the Daily Double, be audacious. I've seen literature professors be in the English Lit category, hit a Daily Double in the $800 box, assume the question will be too difficult, and only wager $500. Give me a break! The clue itself is worth more than that, so why not take a chance? I don't criticize the contestants for what they do, because being on national television can be unnerving, but "nothing ventured, nothing gained" is a cliché that should be stamped on the foreheads of all *Jeopardy!* contestants.

Wagering in Final Jeopardy! is based upon the principle that you get to keep the money only if you are the champion, so that focuses your approach. If players are in contention going into Final Jeopardy! they must assess their positions. If they are well ahead, they can wager enough to win by one dollar, assuming they guess incorrectly and their closest opponent guesses correctly. If the leaders mathematically can't be caught, they sometimes wager very little, ensuring they will keep their current stake. If the race is close, some contestants make their wagers by calculating how much it will take to win if all contestants answer incorrectly, operating under the assumption that the leader will wager enough to win by one dollar if the second-place player wagers his or her entire amount.

The bottom line is this: Bet to win. Don't bet to tie, as some contestants do, because the player you tie today might beat you tomorrow. Some contestants bet to finish second, since second-place prizes are better than those for third. There are all kinds of exceptions to rules, but the most successful *Jeopardy!* contestants are the ones who go for the win.

What are you writing at the podium during the show?

I have a paper grid in front of me that matches the game board, imprinted with the identical material. As the game progresses, I cross off the boxes that are used up, just to keep track of what's going on, to make sure I don't read the wrong clue when one is chosen. We're all creatures of habit, used to reading from the top of a column toward the bottom. Sometimes contestants take that route, and sometimes they don't. I've got to keep up with them. When a contestant chooses a box, our computer operator backstage has to send the right material to the game board, and our director has to focus in on the right box, and I'd better be reading the correct material. And all of this must happen within a second. When a contestant starts skipping all over the board, we all have to work a little harder.

Ever received criticism about how you host the show?

One comment that's come up in letters more than any other is from our older viewers who write to tell me that when a contestant who has been doing well misses a question, I tend to lower my voice when I correct them. And it's true. When a contestant misses a question that causes everyone in the studio and at home to groan, I try to soften the blow a bit by saying, "You were probably thinking of . . ." or "You misspoke slightly. I'm sure you wanted to say this. . . ." That kind of thing. I don't want to make the contestants feel silly or embarrassed. In everyday life, when we have to deliver bad news, our voices usually soften. Adding to this is the fact that when I'm reading the clue, I'm looking down at the sheet on the podium, which means I'm speaking directly into my microphone. But when I'm looking at the contestants I'm speaking slightly away from the microphone, and this definitely affects the audio level. So this is something I'm aware of and will endeavor to change.

Is Jeopardy! easier or harder than it used to be in the Art Fleming days?

This question has been kicked around quite a bit, and the consensus is that the show is more difficult now. First of all, many of the people who believe the show is easier now are fans of the show from the early days, but they were teenagers in the 1960s and, presumably, they know more now than they did then, so they are better players.

One person we asked about this is Burns Cameron, the all-time money winner from the 1960s. Burns never lost on *Jeopardy!* and never really came too close to losing. In fact, he was such a good player, he was invited to represent the United States in an international English-speaking quiz-show championship. "I think the show is harder for the most part now," reports Burns. "The material is tough and the fact that no one can ring in until Alex finishes reading the answer means everyone has an equal chance to consider the correct question. In the old days, if you had a great ability to read quickly and process that information, you had a jump on your opponents."

When *Jeopardy!* returned to the air in 1984, there was some concern on the part of stations that the material was simply too difficult for viewers, that our audience in the evening was so much larger than the old morning show that we had to appeal to a lower common denominator. Well, you be the judge, but when you consider that fact that only 10 percent of the applicants pass the initial test, we have to believe our show is sufficiently challenging.

When you're out in public, do people fire questions at you?

Sometimes. Mostly its very good-natured. Occasionally a person will spot me in an airport and think, Aha! The host of *Jeopardy!* Let me nail him with this question! They come at me with pretty obscure stuff. But having hosted the show six years and produced it for three, sometimes I surprise them with an answer.

How would you do as a contestant?

Since I'm now eligible for the Seniors Tournament, I would probably do okay. Against bright young people with good reflexes, I'd get buried, simply for the reason that as you get older your mind tends to be more selective about the things it's going to remember and will push to the rear things that it's not particularly interested in remembering. To play *Jeopardy!* really well your recall has to be almost indiscriminate.

What's your schedule on game days?

First of all, it's a long day, because we'll tape five shows in one day. I arrive at the studio about nine in the morning, take care of correspondence and general business for an hour, then meet with the producer and the research staff to review the game material. I study each answer and question to see if there is anything I find confusing, and I check my pronunciations. Sometimes the researchers take perverse delight in throwing foreign expressions at me that will be tough to pronounce. Welsh kills me. So I go over the games and check out the Final Jeopardy!s, making certain there aren't clues in one game that will influence a fact in another game. Remember, all the contestants for five shows are there watching the tapings, so we must make certain game material doesn't conflict.

If I have a question about the material, perhaps pertaining to our use of it several months ago, we go to the computer and cross-refer. For instance, if the question pertains to Napoleon, we can summon all Napoleon material and quickly check it out.

After the games are checked, I head down to makeup and get ready for the first program. We'll do three shows with a brief break in between each, stop for dinner, then return for the final two tapings. I'm out of there by eight at night.

Do you talk with the contestants off the air?

Never before the show, only briefly after the show. I do say a few words during a commercial. The problem is this: Since I have studied the game material before the show, and I have the answers and questions on my podium, I must avoid interacting with the contestants because of fairness rules. The contestant coordinators keep the players isolated from contact with anyone who might have had access to the game material. And once the show is over, I go to my dressing room, change clothes, and prepare for the next taping. We take only fifteen minutes between tapings, so there isn't much time for socializing.

When a contestant is ruled incorrect on a tough call, do you make that judgment?

The sheet I'm looking at on the podium contains the correct response. If a contestant comes up with something I'm unsure of, I'll glance toward Harry Eisenberg for a nod either way. If Harry is unsure, the producer George Vosburgh makes the decision. If George is undecided, we stop taping the program and our researchers check out the contestant's response. This is a rare occurrence.

What happens if a contestant's response is ruled incorrect, yet he or she is certain it's right?

The contestant is instructed to wait until a commercial break and then consults with a contestant coordinator. The contestant coordinator immediately informs the producer, who has the information checked out. If the contestant is proved correct, the score is adjusted.

What happens more often than the contestant questioning a ruling is a member of the staff hears a response that we hadn't anticipated, and we'll check it out immediately. If the information turns up after the show is completed, and the dollar amount in question would have changed the outcome of the game, the contestant is invited back for another apperance. Again, though, this is rare.

How did the hat collection get started?

A few years ago the chief petty officer from the USS *New Jersey* was in the audience and invited me to visit. I did visit the ship and he gave me a cap, which I wore on the show. I visited other ships, then started receiving hats in the mail, some from the military, others from schools, all kinds of things. Now I've got at least five hundred of them, an entire closetful.

Do contestants have to pay taxes on their winnings?

Does Santa say ho-ho-ho at Christmas? It's ordinary income, and taxed accordingly.

In Other Words

JEOPARDY!

IN OTHER WORDS

IN OTHER WORDS

IN OTHER WORDS

Entering through a sound-collecting organ, then departing through the opposite.

Snag El Toro using his hard boneline projections.

Allow snoozing schnauzers to go undisturbed.

Persons occupying Pyrex haciendas ought not to fling granite objects.

The twenty-fourth letter indicates precise location.

Despondency adores companionship.

Self shall become a simian's father's brother.

A single wicker container should not hold the entire output of thy hen.

A newsweekly is sent airmail at the moment one experiences amusement.

The simpleton's simoleons swiftly skedaddle.

Perpetually place one's prime pedal extremity in advance.

One that takes a pause becomes unfindable.

Strike brad's cranium.

Perform an optical scan previous to execution of a jeté.

Labor with your digits leaving just skeletal remains.

Effortlessly arrive, effortlessly depart.

Pattern assumed by disintegration of an Oreo.

A void of originality exists beneath our class-G star.

Expired *Homo sapiens* don't relate fables.

The person who finances a Scottish musician gets to pick the song played.

An excess of culinary artistes ruins bouillon.

In good shape, like one violin.

A pair is required to perform a Latin American dance characterized by frequent posturing.

One discharge of a .45 amidst absence of light.

Ingest a pair of acetylsalicylic acid tablets, then make my phone bell ring at 7:00 A.M. tomorrow.

Ill tidings cover ground quickly.

Battle combustion by using combustion.

Excuse this person, lad, could yonder object be a train to Tennessee's fourth-largest city?

Precipitation, precipitation, disappear, return on a different $1/365$ of a year.

Homo sapiens bids, the supreme being rids.

JEOPARDY!

IN OTHER WORDS

What is "in one ear and out the other"?

What is "people who live in glass houses shouldn't throw stones"?

What is "I'll be a monkey's uncle"?

What is "a fool and his money are soon parted"?

What is "hit the nail on the head"?

IN OTHER WORDS

What is "take (grab) the bull by the horns"?

What is "X marks the spot"?

What is "don't put all your eggs in one basket"?

What is "always put your best foot forward"?

What is "look before you leap"?

IN OTHER WORDS

What is "let sleeping dogs lie"?

What is "misery loves company"?

What is "time flies when you're having fun"?

What is "he who hesitates is lost"?

What is "work your fingers to the bone"?

What is "easy come, easy go"?

What is "that's the way the cookie crumbles"?

What is "there is nothing new under the sun"?

What is "dead men tell no tales"?

What is "he who pays the piper calls the tune"?

What is "too many cooks spoil the broth"?

What is "fit as a fiddle"?

What is "it takes two to tango"?

What is "a shot in the dark"?

What is "take two aspirins and call me in the morning"?

What is "bad news travels fast"?

What is "fight fire with fire"?

What is "pardon me, boy, is that the Chattanooga Choo-Choo"?

What is "rain, rain, go away, come again another day"?

What is "man proposes, God disposes"?

DOUBLE JEOPARDY!

IN OTHER WORDS	IN OTHER WORDS	IN OTHER WORDS
Placing one's pedal extremity amidst one's oral cavity.	Bonded together you and I are upright, apart you and I collapse.	Unsighted, like the flying mammal.
Comparable to removing an infant's Snickers.	The fourth month's precipitations elicit the fifth month's blooms.	Not in view, not in brain.
Gape wide, small flat seed found on hamburger buns!	At no time gaze at a freely proferred palomino's pearlies.	A comparable location to one's abode does not exist.
Rapidity creates refuse.	A singular despicable Delicious defiles an entire oak caskful.	One graphic impression equals a millenary of sounds with meaning.
Pointless to lacrimate about an accidentally disseminated lacteal substance.	Succeed as one plumbous blimp.	Enunciation is simpler, compared with execution.

IN OTHER WORDS

Tear free with your teeth an amount in excess of your masticating ability.

Canis lupis garbed with *Ovis aries*'s attire.

Traverse Hades as well as a swollen river.

Yale device, Wall Street commodity plus pickle container.

Lave one's grasping organs in respect to an entire extramarital fling.

IN OTHER WORDS

Make one buffoonish inquiry, receive one buffoonish reply.

Did the kitty catch thy organ of taste?

All the epidermis remains on the proboscis I possess.

Adulation makes no inroads.

Welcome, welcome, everyone of our group has arrived.

IN OTHER WORDS (A LA DISNEY)

"Seven little men help a girl."

"The wooden boy who became real."

"The girl with the see-through shoes."

"Puppies taken away."

"The amazing flying children."

DOUBLE JEOPARDY!

IN OTHER WORDS	IN OTHER WORDS	IN OTHER WORDS
What is "putting your foot in your mouth"?	What is "united we stand, divided we fall"?	What is "blind as a bat"?
What is "like taking candy from a baby"?	What is "April showers bring (forth) May flowers"?	What is "out of sight, out of mind"?
What is "open sesame"?	What is "don't look a gift horse in the mouth"?	What is "there's no place like home"?
What is "haste makes waste"?	What is "one rotten (bad) apple spoils the whole barrel (bunch)"?	What is "a picture is worth a thousand words"?
What is "no use crying over spilt milk"?	What is "go over like a lead balloon"?	What is "easier said than done"?

What is "bite off more than you can chew"?

What is "ask a silly question and get a silly answer"?

What is *"Snow White and the Seven Dwarfs"*?

What is "a wolf in sheep's clothing"?

What is "cat got your tongue"?

What is *"Pinocchio"*?

What is "(go) through hell and high water"?

What is "no skin off my nose"?

What is *"Cinderella"*?

What is "lock, stock, and barrel"?

What is "flattery will get you nowhere"?

What is *"101 Dalmatians"*?

What is "wash your hands of the whole affair"?

What is "hail, hail, the gang's all here"?

What is *"Peter Pan"*?

FINAL JEOPARDY!

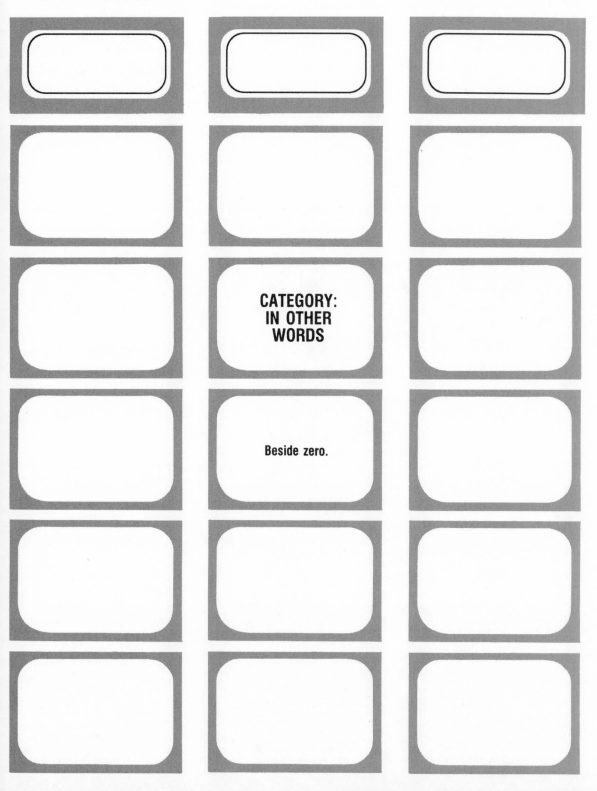

CATEGORY:
IN OTHER
WORDS

Beside zero.

FINAL JEOPARDY!

What is "next to nothing"?

Announcer Johnny Gilbert. (© *1990 King World/Steve Crise*)

The Booth—Director Dick Schneider in striped shirt. (© *1990 King World/Steve Crise*)

Alex with Philipe Risoli, host of the French version of *Jeopardy!* (© *1990 King World/ Steve Crise*)

Alex Trebek. (© *1990 King World/Steve Crise*)

Roundtable meeting: *left to right* (*seated*)—researchers Frederik Pohl, IV, and Kathy Easterling, Alex, Producer George Vosburgh, Editorial Associate Producer Harry Eisenberg; *standing*—Susanne Stone, Debbie Griffin. (© *1990 King World/Steve Crise*)

Stage Manager John Lauderdale familiarizing College Week contestants with the set. (© *1990 King World/Steve Crise*)

Hollywood Center Studios, Stage One, the *Jeopardy!* set. (© *1990 King World/Steve Crise*)

Game board operator Doris Montes. (© *1990 King World/Steve Crise*)

Behind the *Jeopardy!* board. (© *1990 King World/Steve Crise*)

Jeopardy! contestants at work. (*King World*)

Jeopardy! contestants at work. (*King World*)

The *Jeopardy!* set, 1965. (*Fred Wostbrock Archives*)

Merv Griffin created *Jeopardy!* in the dining room of his New York apartment in 1964.

The "A (& Q)" Team

We produce 230 shows per year, and each show contains sixty-one Jeopardy!, Double Jeopardy!, and Final Jeopardy! "answers"; that's 14,030 answers per year, folks. Consider the fact that *Jeopardy!* has twenty seasons behind it, and we're approaching 300,000 answers in hundreds of categories.

"Every day we had at least one new category," remembers *Jeopardy!*'s first producer, Bob Rubin. "We put it in the first column of each game. Of course, we were starting from scratch so the world was open to us. We did every state, almost every country, different types of history, all the basics. And we made sure to have fun with it all. We'd take what basically is history and turn it into Wild West, Cops and Robbers, that sort of thing. Categories that tended to scare contestants included United Nations and Explorers, so we wouldn't book those more than once a month. The Bible also stopped some good players right in their tracks, but we made certain the questions were balanced between the Old and New Testaments so that we wouldn't be accused of favoring anybody. I liked the show-business categories, because we could have so much fun with them. And people still talk about Creepers and Crawlers, and Potent Potables."

Currently, we have a staff of twelve who create, verify, and assemble the *Jeopardy!* game boards. Before an answer appears on the air, it has gone through six stages of checking. Editorial Associate Producer Harry Eisenberg describes the process: "We either assign categories to researchers, or they come up with them. Then each answer must be sourced twice, with all the information and verification put on a card. Then I edit the category, obviously checking for a balance between the difficulty of the material and the dollar value assigned to it. Once I'm finished with that, the material is kicked back to the research department, and another researcher verifies all the information. We try to anticipate all the possible and likely responses, and research each of them. Once a game is assembled it goes to George Vosburgh, the producer, for review, and he will edit the material and, perhaps, ask for further verification. On show day, we take a final look at the material with Alex, and we check inquiries that he makes before taking the material to air."

Still, contestants can confound us. In a Religion category, one answer was, "The territory of a church under the jurisdiction of a Bishop." Our question was, "What is a diocese?" But the contestant's response was, "What is a bishopric?" During the next commercial, the staff checked the dictionary and learned that the definition of a bishopric was "the diocese of a bishop." After the break, we credited the contestant with a correct answer.

Do we make mistakes? Of course, but not many, and we are scrupulous about correcting our errors. Source books make mistakes; sometimes two books have been wrong about similar information. We had one Henry VIII answer where four different encyclopedias disagreed on precise dates. So in a case like that one we'll go for the essence of the information and mention the decade but not the exact year.

When a dispute arises during a show about an answer, we'll try and settle it there and then, stopping the tape if necessary. For example, a contestant once raised an objection to an answer involving the length of a term for federal judges. The correct response was 'What is life?' but the contestant was adamant that the term was only for six years, despite our published references. Since we were taping at 6:00 P.M. PST, we couldn't call Washington, D.C., but we did reach the federal court in Hawaii and verified our information on the spot.

Sometimes, in our pursuit of accuracy, eyebrows get raised. Sandy Sycafoose was researching a question about the location of the CIA, and had come across sources offering differing answers. "So I called the CIA," relates Sandy, "and told them who I was and what I wanted to know. The woman who answered my call seemed uncertain about my request and put me on hold. After a while a male voice picked up the phone, and again I explained that I worked on *Jeopardy!* and wanted to verify the location of the CIA. He hemmed and hawed and finally told me, 'We don't handle that here, you'll have to call public relations.' I called that department, presented my case, and was told, 'We'll have to get back to you on that.' Two days later I received a call informing me that Langley, Virginia, was the correct location of the CIA, but I'm sure by then I'd been run through a computer background check."

In certain instances, our research has lead to multiple answers to very specific questions. Researcher Steven Dorfman, in a Food and Drink category, included this double-answer: "In the song 'Lola' (L-O-L-A, Lola), the champagne tasted like this Cola (C-O-L-A, Cola)." The correct questions were "What is Coca-Cola?" or "What is cherry cola?"

"The reason we had two possible responses was one of the tougher things I ever had to track down," says Steven. "There seemed to be different versions recorded by the Kinks of the same song. I called their record company, who put me on to the president of the Kinks' fan club, who couldn't answer my question. Finally, I found the band's manager in London and learned that when the song was originally recorded, the BBC refused to play it since it contained a plug for Coca-Cola. So the Kinks rerecorded the song using cherry cola instead of Coke. But in concert, the Kinks continued using Coca-Cola, and recordings exist of both versions. When our show aired, we got many letters asking for an explanation."

"There is no happy medium as to whether a contestant's response is acceptable," says Harry Eisenberg. "There's no comfortable middle ground. If we're too strict we can be perceived as unfair, but being too lenient violates the intellectual atmosphere of the show. We have to make judgments about marginal responses. Do we accept Sally Fields as correct, when Sally Field is her name? If we accept an imprecise question from one player, we at that same moment deprive the other two players of their opportunity to respond and earn points. Being lenient, for whatever reason, opens us up to charges of favoritism. I have often said that judging on *Jeopardy!* is not an exact science, but our players seem to feel they are being treated fairly. If they have a complaint, we listen to it and try to resolve the matter during a commercial break before continuing with the game. The producer has the final word on the subject, but we try to be prepared. If the contestant has the name correct, but the pronunciation is off, we'll be more lenient than in the case of Field vs. Fields."

That is not always possible, of course, and there are times when a contestant will go to great lengths to question our judgment. We had a Final Jeopardy! about the only number that cannot be expressed as a Roman numeral. "What is '0'?" is the correct response. All three contestants got it right. Two of them wrote "zero" and the third wrote "0." Several weeks after that taping, I received a forty-page dissertation from one of the contestants who took the position that the players who wrote *zero* should have been ruled incorrect, that *zero* is not a number, only a word. His letter was replete with footnotes and cross-references that would have humbled a Jesuit scholar. However, I wrote him back stating that the basic response we had been seeking was fulfilled by *zero,* but that his letter was worthy of publication in an appropriate academic journal.

From the inception of the show, Merv has meant for an ideal *Jeopardy!* answer to be a declarative sentence—"He was the first president of the United States"—leading to an equally unambiguous response. And he intended for the material to entertain as well as inform. "I want the viewer to say, 'Wow, I didn't know that!" Merv explains. "The clue should contain something odd that points the contestant in the right direction."

Associate Producer Harry Eisenberg offers an example under the category of Presidents: "All presidents but James Buchanan had one." The question was, "What is a wife?"

"We call it the 'crux and frill,'" states Harry. "After all these years of *Jeopardy!* the crux of an answer appears again and again, such as information about the presidents, but the frill is what makes it entertaining. For instance, under Presidential Ailments, we ran 'A confirmed hypochondriac, he was in constant pain because of his false teeth.' It's a way of using an answer that we've done hundreds of times, George Washington."

"We always enjoy making history and other so-called academic subjects fun for the viewer," says researcher Kathy Easterling. "An ordinary question can be livened up with just a few extra words. For example, in one of my Ancient Rome categories, I could have written, 'He led a slave revolt in 73 B.C.'—'Who was Spartacus?' But it's more fun to write it this way, 'This gladiator-school dropout led a slave revolt in 73 B.C.' "

It is part of the show's style to "back load" the clues. We've found it's more interesting for the viewer, and helpful to the contestant, to include the most essential information at the end of the clue. For example, again in the Ancient Rome category, "The first Roman circus, it was also the largest"—we hope this leads the contestant to "What was the Circus Maximus?"

The *Jeopardy!* researchers maintain that even in categories that might seem obscure, like Nuclear Physics, the clues will lead contestants to the responses. "Sometimes," maintains Kathy Easterling, "if a contestant catches on to certain similarities within the questions in a given category, he or she will have a much better chance of coming up with correct responses. For example, here are a few questions drawn from our From the French category: (1) This word for one type of hairdo derives from *bouffer,* 'to puff up'; (2) From its name, you'd think this private room is a good place to *bouder,* or 'pout'; (3) Derived from an old Provençal word meaning 'storehouse,' it now means 'a small, chic shop.'

"Of course, in order, the correct responses are bouffant, boudoir, and boutique. A sharp contestant would notice this after the first two questions and would have a good chance of running the category. And this is another reason it's easier to play our game well if you pick the answers in order, instead of hopscotching around the board. You have a much better chance of doing well if you follow the given pattern. Chuck Forrest liked to skip around, but he was an exceptional player."

Researcher Steven Dorfman adds, "By starting from the top of a category you might eliminate certain answers from the big-money windows. This can help you later. If one of the first correct responses to something is 'What is France?' you can be sure it won't be used again in the $1000 slot. Sometimes contestants do well in difficult categories simply by having eliminated other possible responses."

The exception to not skipping around, of course, is if there is little time left in the game and you need to make up a large dollar amount. Also, if you are in doubt about a response, the researchers maintain that your first impulse is usually the correct one. Don't out-think yourself. "If the clue includes the identification 'French emperor,' " explains Kathy, "you can bet we're looking for Napoleon. Go for the obvious and, in most cases, you'll be right."

In terms of preparation for the show, the researchers tend to agree with the contestants that you can't cram for *Jeopardy!* "Most of the material is stuff you either know or don't know," says Harry. "Even if you know it, that doesn't mean you can always recall it during the show. Some of the highest test scores came from contestants who bombed out during taping. It involves a certain knack, an ability to know the style of answers and questions. That's why our best advice to prospective contestants is that they faithfully watch the show. If you plan to study, then it should be presidents, states, world capitals. And geography. You'd be amazed how many people don't know their rivers and mountains."

Or that the Kinks recorded two versions of "Lola"!

The researchers tend to be as varied as the contestants. We look for a balance of interests. "Perhaps an English major with an off-the-wall minor," says George Vosburgh. "And they have to be able to pass the contestant test. After that, we have them do some sample categories and judge their feel for the style of our material."

Harry Eisenberg, who heads up the research staff, earned a master's degree in history, then worked as a copier salesman. "I made a good living doing that, but wanted to be a writer. I wrote a screenplay and came to Hollywood. That was in 1984 and upon arrival I heard about the return of *Jeopardy!* I knew immediately that working on the show was something I wanted to do. When I was in high school, I used to come home during lunch hour to watch the Art Fleming version of the show."

Another prolific researcher, Steven Dorfman was a successful game-show contestant prior to signing on with *Jeopardy!*, having won five thousand dollars on a show called *Battlestars* (a show hosted by one Alex Trebek).

Researcher Carlo Panno had been a contestant on *Jeopardy!* in 1978. He won one game, but lost the next day on a missed Daily Double. However, when he was backstage, he hit it off with a female contestant. "The contestant coordinator noticed that we were getting along. She knew it even before we did," recalls Carlo, "and for that reason they put us on different shows. But we became friends and, several years later, we got married!"

One can only assume that Carlo did not fail to propose in the form a question.

Men of Note

JEOPARDY!

SINATRA

He did his own fight scenes when he appeared on this TV P.I.'s show in February 1987.

The Arizona radio station Sinatra bought in 1989 was dubbed KFAS, the FAS standing for this.

As Joey Evans in this 1957 film, Sinatra belted out "The Lady Is a Tramp."

Sinatra made his first record in July 1939 as a vocalist for this trumpeter's band.

Dying in this film, Sinatra warns Prew, "Watch out for Fatso. He'll try to crack you."

SIMON AND GARFUNKEL

Their first number-one hit, it begins: "Hello darkness, my old friend."

Where you'd go for "parsley, sage, rosemary, and thyme."

This song plaintively asks "Where have you gone, Joe DiMaggio?"

In "Slip Slidin' Away" Simon was backed up by this country group known for "Elvira."

They first recorded under names borrowed from this cartoon pair.

THE BOSS

Until recently, it was the band that backs up the Boss.

Though he's never had a number-one single, this song boogied on up to number two in 1984.

In May 1985, he broke many female hearts by marrying this actress.

Bruce was indeed born in the U.S.A.—in this town, in fact.

In October 1975 the Boss graced the covers of these two weekly magazines simultaneously.

THE BEACH BOYS

Sport mentioned in the titles of their first three top hits.

As lead singer, Al Jardine asked for this girl's "help" to get his old girl out of his heart.

When Brian Wilson stopped touring in 1964, he was replaced by this "Rhinestone Cowboy."

Cabinet officer summoned to the White House April 7, 1983, where he was convinced to un-ban the Beach Boys.

One of their two top-ten hits whose titles consisted of one word repeated three times.

ELVIS

He appeared on Steve Allen's TV show after this man, on opposite Allen, wouldn't have him.

The single "Don't Be Cruel" featured this animal on its jacket.

His hit "It's Now or Never" was adapted from this Italian song.

City in which, as a present for his mother, Elvis cut his first record ever.

While in the army, Elvis did his basic training at this Texas base.

KENNY ROGERS

Home base for Kenny and family is a ranch in this "peachy" state.

His wife Marianne was once a regular on this country comedy TV show.

His only number-one pop hit as a solo artist was this one-word title song of 1980 written by Lionel Richie.

One of the three female artists with whom Kenny Rogers has had a top-ten pop hit.

With the First Edition in 1967, Kenny "just dropped in to see" this.

JEOPARDY!

SINATRA	SIMON AND GARFUNKEL	THE BOSS
Who is (Thomas) Magnum?	What is "The Sounds of Silence"?	What is the "E" Street Band?
What is Francis (Frank) Albert Sinatra?	What is "Scarborough Fair"?	What is "Dancing in the Dark"?
What is *Pal Joey?*	What is "Mrs. Robinson"?	Who is Julianne Phillips?
Who was Harry James?	Who are the Oak Ridge Boys?	What is Freehold, New Jersey?
What is *From Here to Eternity?*	Who are Tom and Jerry?	What are *Time* and *Newsweek?*

THE BEACH BOYS	ELVIS	KENNY ROGERS
What is surfing?	Who was Ed Sullivan?	What is Georgia?
Who is Rhonda?	What is a hound dog?	What is *Hee Haw?*
Who is Glen Campbell?	What is "O Sole Mio"?	What is "Lady"?
Who is James Watt?	What is Memphis?	Who are Kim Carnes, Sheena Easton, or Dolly Parton?
What is "Fun, Fun, Fun" or "Dance, Dance, Dance"?	What is Fort Hood?	What is "what condition my condition is in"?

DOUBLE JEOPARDY!

THE BEATLES

He pointed out his "classic nose" in a commercial for Classic wine cooler.

Three of the first four Billboard number-one hits for the Beatles had this word in their titles.

It's "waiting . . . ," "hoping . . . ," "coming. . . ,," and "dying to take you away."

On March 21, 1987, four Beatles albums held the top four positions on this new Billboard chart.

Song that tells the story of Desmond and Molly Jones.

THE BEATLES

He was their guru.

In 1971 he organized two concerts for Bangladesh at New York's Madison Square Garden.

Though "Love Me Do" was their first hit single in Britain, this song was their first to top U.S. charts.

He was the Beatles' drummer before Ringo.

Only Beatle never to have been divorced.

THE BEATLES

His first name is really James, but he uses his middle name.

Among songs on his first solo album were *Gat Kirwani*, *Fabla and Pakanavj* and *Guru Vandana*.

The girl in "Lucy in the Sky with Diamonds" has this type of eyes.

The *Harmony Encyclopedia of Rock* says their name was inspired by this American group with an insect name.

While they recorded their first album in less than a day, this mid-1967 album took months and months.

THE BEATLES

Color of the cover of the album officially titled *The Beatles.*

The only day of the week not mentioned in "Lady Madonna"; maybe three syllables were hard to rhyme.

In August 1962 he was kicked out of the group.

Since *Sgt. Pepper* was released in 1967, this was the year Pepper taught the band to play.

Tommy Smothers, Timothy Leary, and others joined this Beatle and his new wife in "Give Peace a Chance."

THE BEATLES

The German version of this hit is titled "Sie Liebt Dich."

Working title for film *A Hard Day's Night*, it became title for an "incredible simulation" instead.

They agreed as kids that all of their songs would be credited to both, no matter who wrote what.

Poem that inspired "I Am the Walrus."

Called "Fifth Beatle" on 1969's "Get Back," he shared label billing with the Fab Four.

THE BEATLES

Alphabetically first of films featuring the Beatles, it was also their first film.

He reminisced about the good old days in "When We Were Fab."

The last name of this "Fifth Beatle" was Kaufman.

You can find "Lucy in the Sky" in a sky made of this sweet substance.

In a 1965 hit, it's what came "suddenly."

DOUBLE JEOPARDY!

THE BEATLES	THE BEATLES	THE BEATLES
Who is Ringo Starr?	Who is the Maharishi Mahesh Yogi?	Who is James Paul McCartnery?
What is "Love"?	Who is George Harrison?	Who is George Harrison?
What is "The Magical Mystery Tour"?	What is "I Want to Hold Your Hand"?	What are kaleidoscope?
What is the Top CDs?	Who is Peter (Pete) Best?	Who were the Crickets?
What is "Ob-La-Di, Ob-La-Da"?	Who is Paul McCartney?	What is *Sgt. Pepper's (Lonely Hearts Club Band)*?

THE BEATLES

THE BEATLES

THE BEATLES

What is white?

What is "She Loves You"?

What is *A Hard Day's Night?*

What is Saturday?

What is *Beatlemania?*

Who is George Harrison?

Who is Pete Best?
(DNA: Stu Sutcliffe)

Who are Lennon and McCartney?

Who was Murray the K?

What is 1947?

What is "The Walrus and the Carpenter"?

What is marmalade?

Who is John Lennon?

Who is Billy Preston?

What is "Yesterday"?

FINAL JEOPARDY!

**CATEGORY:
THE BEATLES**

Type of apple in the Apple Records logo.

FINAL JEOPARDY!

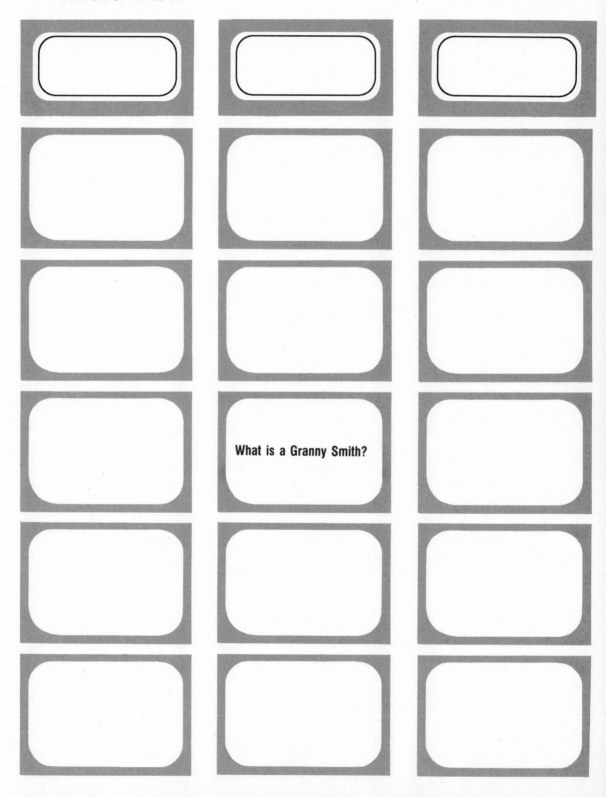

What is a Granny Smith?

The Contestants—Who *Are* These People?

One downed twelve cups of black coffee minutes before airtime. Another spent a weekend reading the World Almanac aloud to his dachsund. Several have videotaped the show and practiced buzzing by using the pause button on a remote control device. And one gentleman stopped at a church on the way to the studio to light a votive candle for luck, then found himself praying in the form of a question.

These are *Jeopardy!* contestants, and in the fiercely competitive world of television game shows, they are the elite, the high priests and priestesses of knowledge, information, and trivia. *Jeopardy!* contestants are to game shows what the Green Berets are to the military, and like the Green Berets, they take no prisoners. Many can't get an invitation to play a friendly game of Trivial Pursuit, because they never lose. Or they are brought in as ringers, just to dazzle the average folk. Some have Ph.D.s from prestigious universities and are successful attorneys, scientists, or State Department officials. Others never graduated from high school; waiters and cab drivers have been *Jeopardy!* champions. Most of these are quick to tell you that they don't watch game shows, and have only applied to appear on one game show in their lives, and that show is, of course, *Jeopardy!*

To become a contestant on *Jeopardy!* you are not required to dress up like a tuna melt, leap in the air, or reveal the sexual quirks of your mate. Having a genius-level I.Q. won't be enough, either, though it wouldn't hurt. To succeed on *Jeopardy!* it takes more than intelligence, luck, and personality, but having all three is a good start. Contestants must instantly access their memory on subjects as diverse as Howdy Doody and Shakespeare, and do so with thousands of dollars at stake and millions of viewers judging every response. And these contestants must be able to summon facts while two competitors, equally gifted, are straining to do the same thing, only faster.

Sound difficult? It is. Sound fun? If so, you're a candidate.

And there are rewards. Most important, the satisfaction of knowing how you measure up to the best and brightest of your fellow *Jeopardy!* fanatics. Plus cash. Sometimes lots of it. *Jeopardy!*'s biggest winner, Chuck Forrest, waltzed home in 1986 with $172,000 and global bragging rights. Many contestants have won chunks of money sizeable enough to alter the course of their lives.

But it is a slippery path that winds from your living room, den, or wherever it is you watch the show, to our stage on Sunset Boulevard in Hollywood.

Consider these facts: Susanne Thurber, the show's contestant coordinator, reports that 250,000 people apply for the show annually. Of those, 15,000 are chosen to take the first screening exam; 1,500 qualify as contestants, and only 500 finally make it to air. Of those making to the show, fifteen make it to the Tournament of Champions.

The odds aren't great, but where else can you win $175,000 playing a game that gives you the answers?

MOTHER KNOWS BEST OR HOW I ENDED UP ON *JEOPARDY!*

Most contestants who try out and qualify for *Jeopardy!* have watched it for years, harboring the belief that they could do as well at it as anyone else. Others decide it might be a way of picking up easy money. For some, it takes a nudge to move from viewer to participant.

"I was a fan of the old show," recalls Bruce Naegeli, law library clerk from Phoenix, Arizona. "I'd spent a summer on the graveyard shift working in an aluminum factory, and I used to watch the show while I ate my dinner after work, which was late morning. My mother is the world's biggest fan of the show, and for years had been after me to try out for it. 'You know all that stuff,' she'd tell me, 'why are you just walking around with it in your head and not making any money off of it?'

"In March of 1987 they were doing a search in our area, so my mother called the number, then presented it to me as a fait accompli. So

I wouldn't have to hear about it for the rest of my life, I decided to take the test. I passed, got on the show, and ended up winning over eighty-three thousand dollars.

"I'll never win another argument with my mother for as long as she lives, because whenever I disagree with her on anything, she can remind me of how gloriously right she was about *Jeopardy!*"

Teachers sometimes intercede on behalf of bright students, as in the case of 1988 Teen Tournament winner Michael Block. "My first day as a senior in high school I went down to see my faculty advisor regarding a problem with my schedule. Before I could get into that, she said she wanted me to send a postcard to *Jeopardy!* and apply as a contestant. I didn't do it but she kept bothering me about it until I did. Obviously, it worked out nicely for me."

The personable Bob Verini, 1987 Tournament of Champions winner to the tune of $146,000, first tried getting on the show when he was thirteen years old. "It was the Art Fleming days, 1966, and I looked older than I was. Only after the test was over did they ask my age, and at the time they didn't have Teen Tournaments, so I wasn't eligible. Evidently, I had done pretty well and might have been chosen. When the show came back in 1984, I was ready to try again, and the rest is history."

Another winner, Eric Larsen, took a businesslike approach to trying out for *Jeopardy!* "I had been accepted to graduate school, but was unemployed. So I persuaded my mom and dad to finance a trip to Los Angeles in exchange for a percentage of any winnings on the show. Basically, I made a deal and it worked out."

Eric's approach was not unlike that of Jeff Richmond, who won fifty-eight thousand dollars in 1988. At the time he had applied and been accepted to law school, but wasn't looking forward to a starving student budget. "I was trying to figure out where I could get some money, and *Jeopardy!* was one of the first things that came to mind." And, judging by his winnings, not the last.

"My husband, son, and daughter all kept saying, 'Oh, Mom, you need to try out for this,' " recalls 1989 Senior Tournament finalist Ouida Rellstab, a teacher from Louisiana. "They kept telling me how good I was at the game. Even my mother was after me about it, and I'd tell her I would have to go all the way to California for it, and I don't do that sort of stuff. I tried out just for the fun of it, and to get my family to shut up! And I was certain that by being on the show I'd prove to my family I wasn't that great, and they'd stop teasing me. I never expected things to turn out the way they did."

WHAT I DID FOR LOVE (AND MONEY)

You know the look. I finish reading the answer and a contestant buzzes. The camera moves in for a close-up, and we see that blend of terror, frustration, and blankness: the contestant knows the correct question is trapped in his brain, a synapse away from the lips, but the words, at least the right words, are suddenly as elusive as manners at a frat party.

It can be like meeting your favorite movie star; you know exactly what you'd tell them if you just had the chance, but if the elevator door opens and there stands The Star, it's amazing how often one's brain takes an unexpected vacation. Anyone who has appeared on *Jeopardy!* will tell you that strange things happen once the lights go on, the theme music plays, and the first answer is revealed. Even to the best of them.

Many contestants have had the experience of seeing and hearing an answer, only to have their minds play tricks on them. Like Frank Spangenberg, who holds the all-time one-week record winnings total of $102,000. "This has to do with the difference I experienced playing the game for real, as opposed to playing it in my living room. When you're on the show, you go to automatic pilot, as it were, hoping that your brain is giving you the answer, your finger is pushing the button, and your mouth is speaking the answer correctly. It all has to work together. At home, you're relaxed and this works. On the show I found myself a few times giving wrong answers, and sometimes right ones, automatically, and I thought to myself, 'I know that's wrong, why did I say that?' For instance, the category was Geography, and the answer was 'Salvation Army headquarters located in this capital.' The correct question, of course, is 'what is London?'" recalls Frank. "I happen to know quite a bit about the history of the Salvation Army; there is a Salvation Army hospital near my home, and I know about General Booth and the history of this organization. I heard Alex read 'Salvation Army' and I looked at the printed words on the board. But I read it as 'Red Cross.' I don't have the slightest idea why I did that. I wanted to say Geneva, because that is the headquarters of the Red Cross, but not the capital of Switzerland. So I said Zurich, and I'm sure everyone thought I was crazy. To this day I cannot tell you why I read that answer as Red Cross."

Things worked the other way for Frank, too. "There was a Final Jeopardy! answer about the headquarters of the Welch's Corporation in Massachusetts. I had no idea. But my thoughts went like this: 'They're famous for grape jelly, which they make from Concord grapes. Maybe it's Concord, Mass.' And I was right, so you can pull things from the air like that if you study the answer and relax."

One hundred thousand dollars later, Frank feels quite relaxed.

Other contestants are shocked to pull correct questions from nowhere in categories they thought they knew nothing about. Roy Halliday won sixty-two thousand dollars in 1987–88, and put on one of the great sprints to the finish in the show's history. Roy taped his entire week of shows in one day, and by the fifth show felt his brain ready to short-circuit.

"I had literally sort of wigged out after a while. It was the fifth show of the day and I was on auto-pilot. I was behind badly by the time we were in the Double Jeopardy! round, and Alex announced there was only one minute to go. The only category left was Southern Authors, which we'd all been avoiding. I took a deep breath, knew I had to make up money, and started from the bottom and ran the category working back toward the top. I leap-frogged from last to first place, which let me win. Somebody later told me that for those last sixty seconds, my entire face changed. I was like a machine doing nothing more than pressing the buzzer and spitting out answers.

"I have no idea where my knowledge of Southern Authors came from. The bizarre thing is that a lot of times during the show an answer will pop up, you'll press the buzzer and give the correct question, and the back of your mind is asking, 'Why do I know that? From where?' I think the people who do well on this show frankly are ones who aren't in it for the money, who are simply doing it because they've been watching the show for years and love it. That reason, on some level, frees up the mind enough to allow everything from the subconscious to come forward. *Jeopardy!* is psychotherapy."

Once you're picked as a contestant, does it help to study? I'm asked this question frequently, and I tend to agree with the contestants who feel that studying clogs the brain rather than relaxing it; if you don't know how to dance by the time you get to the party, it's unlikely you'll learn once the music starts. "I didn't really study outside material," Michael Rankins, a sixty-thousand-dollar winner, remembers. "I just watched the show a lot and tried to get a feel for the game. The main thing that helps me is that I've got an incredible memory for useless information. My wife could ask me something she told me five minutes before and I've already forgotten it. But I pick up little facts here and there and they stick. I've got a good fact-based memory, but not a good event-based memory."

Jeopardy!'s winningest contest, Chuck Forrest, a political officer with the U.S. Department of State, says, "Reading trivia books is a waste of time. When I was headed for the Tournament of Champions I memorized all the Oscar winners, since that is a common category. Of course, it never came up."

Michael Block, 1988 Teen Tournament winner, took the contestant test in Pittsburgh, and recalls the bizarre scene he encountered there. "I showed up at the hotel where the test was being given, and packed into the lobby were two hundred kids reading almanacs, cramming. I was reading Kafka for English class, just doing my homework. And I was shocked, because I don't think you get much from that approach. I think *Jeopardy!* just tests your overall education and everything you've encountered in life."

Five-time winner Larry McKnight agrees. "When I went to the taping there was a contestant backstage flipping through a copy of the *World Almanac.* But you can't cram for it. It has to be that you hear an answer and a light goes off in your subconscious that you know the question, so you buzz in and let the question rise to the surface. Cramming doesn't do that for you. It doesn't put the information down deep enough in the brain." Eugene Finnerman picked up seventy thousand dollars in 1987, and observes that *Jeopardy!* doesn't lend itself to studying. "The category could just as easily be on Leave It to Beaver as the French Revolution, so there's no preparation in terms of breaking open the books. In hindsight, if there is a preparation for the show, it's getting a feel for the way *Jeopardy!* questions are constructed; often, they have implicit answers within them, or are phrased in a fashion that gives you a clue. I'd advise a contestant to avoid hangovers, stay alert, and try not to let nerves overcome you. In terms of memorizing encyclopedias, no."

Joel Sacks of Maryland racked up over fifty thousand dollars in 1988. He considered studying for the show, and decided not to, though felt a wave of worry about his decision. "That was my great fear, that I'd get on the show, do poorly, then really blame myself for not having studied. All the other contestants there with me had studied. My only strategy was not to end up negative in the first round. All I wanted to do was hang in so that I could reach Final Jeopardy! and still be in contention.

"In terms of preparation," Joel continues, "some contestants had gone all the way to Hollywood to try out in the studio so that they could see it before their appearance, get a feel for it. They wanted to prepare that way for their nerves. Looking back, I would tell future contestants to just be themselves, don't feel like once they're on the show they've got to put on some kind of act. Once the game starts, you'll forget all about where you are. And it goes by quickly. You don't know that before you're actually on the show, but once the show is on, you just can't believe how fast it goes by. I suppose that comes from all the anticipation. The only real nervous moment comes when you walk into the studio, if you haven't seen it, and there's the real set you've watched on television for years. Once the game starts, you forget about that and the experience flies by."

Many former contestants remark upon the speed with which the games pass once they're in the studio. "When you're at home watching the game," says Jeff Richmond, "you know who's leading and who's behind. But when you're up there, you're oblivious to that. It's the one thing I hadn't really expected, that you can't keep track of the game when you're playing, it just goes by too fast. At commercial breaks you get a chance to look at the board and see who has what. But when the game is on, you just keep trying to come up with the correct questions."

While many champions have done no preparation for their appearances, others found that a bit of preparation paid dividends.

Tournament of Champions winner Bob Verini followed a specific training regimen. "I played the box game and taped the television show, watched it religiously to get down the timing of the questions. For the tournament I brushed up on categories I felt weak in. I needed to memorize the signs of the zodiac, the order of the planets from the sun, basic stuff like that." Only a *Jeopardy!* fan would consider such things basic, but Bob cashed in. "I was pretty weak on American Indians. So I studied. Then during one game I was in third place going into Final *Jeopardy!* The only way for me to win was if I got it right and my opponents got it wrong. The answer was 'War in which Abraham Lincoln and Jefferson Davis first met.' The question is 'What is the Black Hawk War?' That information stuck with me when I studied because it was the only military experience Lincoln had. I got it right and won the game, so my preparation paid off."

"If you watch the show regularly," contends champion Mark Lowenthal, "you know the things you absolutely must know. And those are the things I memorized. Presidents, everything about the states, geography, Oscars. I marked up an almanac with the key stuff, and memorized it all."

The 1965 Tournament of Champions winner, Burns Cameron, is known as the greatest player of the 1960s. He doesn't believe in much preparation, but agrees with Mark Lowenthal that you have to know your U.S. history and states information. "Study the states, the flowers, birds, songs, capitals, all of that. Those categories come up a lot and can go in many directions."

"Being able to quickly associate is more important than just knowing facts," counters Joel Sacks, with fifty-one thousand dollars backing his opinion. "There're always clues in the questions, so you rarely have to know the particular fact. If you have a broad base of knowledge, information, rather than lists of facts, you tend to do well. That's my ability, general information without knowing a lot of specific facts."

And sometimes contestants admit to being plain lucky. Like Ouida Rellstab. "I happened to look at a word the day before taping and remarked, 'I didn't know the Spanish word for yellow is *amarillo,* how interesting.' That turned out to be one of the questions on the show. And I'd been looking for a movie of Stephen Smith, the English poet, to show my honor students while I was away from class, and doggone, that turned out to be a question, too. My son is in Argentina, and I got an Argentina category in the show. So I wasn't surprised by what I knew, I was surprised at the luck I had with the questions. Also, being a teacher, I'm used to telling my students to get the facts before they speak, so maybe some of that rubbed off on me."

Arizona's Bruce Naegeli got a little assist from a coworker. "Prior to being in the tournament, I'd spend my lunch hours with the *World Almanac,* and one of my friends suddenly asked me, 'Where were the Olympics held in 1912?' I didn't have the slightest idea, so all afternoon he kidded me saying anybody who was going to be on *Jeopardy!* should certainly know the location of the 1912 Olympics. Just for fun I turned to the page in the almanac and looked at the list of Olympic sites. It's a brief list, so I memorized it. As it turned out, I won a game in Final Jeopardy! when the answer was 'Only two inhabited continents that have never hosted summer Olympic games.' I mentally ran down the list and came up with Africa and South America. That's one time when memorizing really did pay off."

All contestants agree, however, that one kind of preparation is meaningful, and that pertains to the dreaded buzzer.

Senior champion Peggy Kennedy believes that practicing the buzzer helped her win. "My advice to future contestants is to practice their timing the way I did; my husband made me a little box so I could watch the show at home, push a button, and actually get the feel of it." Many contestants practice by using the remote pause button while watching tapes of the shows.

Winner Roy Holliday employed a less complicated method. "*Jeopardy!* is on twice a day in New York, so I taped both shows for three weeks before I was to appear. Then I'd watch both after dinner, standing in front of the set, since I knew I'd be standing on a podium in the studio, and I used a number-two Phillips screwdriver as my buzzer. I practiced standing, buzzing, and answering.

"One reason, I believe, that we see many duplicate winners on *Jeop-*

ardy! is because there is a definite rhythm to buzzing in. You get used to the cadence of Alex's speech after a while, and you get a sense of how the person in the booth who is flipping the release switch is working off Alex's cadence. And it is a definite rhythm.

"There is one problem that can arise out of this. When I won my five shows, as with other contestants who return for the tournament, many months can pass between appearances. So the serious contestants, the ones for whom winning *Jeopardy!*'s Tournament of Champions was clearly meant to be the highlight of their life, became extremely upset when they learned that during the tournament there was a new person in the booth flipping the release switch on the lockout. All these contestants felt that they'd learned the rhythm when they originally won, and complained that they now had to learn a new person's rhythm. It threw several of them into a spin."

"There's an aspect of the game that's physical," comments architect Leah Greenwald, winner of fifty-eight thousand dollars in 1988, "and it has to do with how fast your neurons fire and how accurately you can get into the proper window of button pressing, not too soon and not too late. I'm not wonderful at buzzing in, but I sort of managed in the regular series because I had enough information in my brain to boost me along. But in the Tournament of Champions, the buzzing hurt me. I'm sure we would all prefer to claim weakness in body rather than in mind, reflexes rather than knowledge. But I did feel it was a handicap for me. That's why when people ask me for advice before appearing, I advise lots of sleep. I have no idea whether reflex speed can be improved, but if it can, then that's what contestants should work on."

Tournament of Champions winner Bob Verini: "Command of the buzzer could come and go so readily that you might be on a roll, the timing just right with the buzzer, and then you could lose it and be off for quite a while. Athletes are familiar with that phenomenon, where they have 'it' for a while, then lose it. Part of winning on the show is rising above that, having enough perspective and sense of humor about it all not to go to pieces when you lose the feel of the buzzer. That's the advice I give, keep your sense of humor when things aren't going your way on the show."

"And don't try to keep careful track of the money," adds Bruce Naegeli. "Only when you hit a Daily Double or are in Final Jeopardy! During the rest of the game don't pay attention to anything but the answer, because it's all going by so fast. If you can do that, then your only worry is the buzzer. I felt like ripping it out of the podium sometimes."

Trying to master the buzzer has done in more than one contestant.

For instance, there was the woman who was buzzing like mad, yet never first. I noticed as the round progressed she was becoming increasingly frustrated, pushing the buzzer harder, faster, and with growing passion. Finally, she was convinced the buzzer was inoperative, because she simply couldn't get in. It was at that point I noticed she was trying to ring in by pressing her marking pen, and not her buzzer.

"The buzzer can definitely give you a hard time," says 1986 Tournament of Champions participant Bruce Seymour. "I found that it was simply a matter of luck, though it did get easier the more games I played. I'd get on a streak and make it in every time, then all of sudden get on another streak where I'd never make it in. So I think an awful lot of *Jeopardy!* is luck. The people you beat are not necessarily dumber or slower than you are. It's the buzzer, the categories, and the questions. My strategy was to avoid the top windows, the one-hundred- and two-hundred-dollar answers. The Daily Doubles almost never appear on top, and they are reasonably important to get, so I'd always start on the second window and work down. My friend Jay Rosenberg, who also appeared on the show, advised me not to guess, it just doesn't pay. Also, I learned not to despair at the end of the first Jeopardy! round, because it's nothing but a warm-up. The Double Jeopardy! round can turn the game 180 degrees very rapidly. That round is the real game."

And Bruce adds his comments about the preparation aspect of the game. "What gives you the best knowledge for *Jeopardy!* are not books so much as newspapers and magazines. They never ask truly detailed questions, they want the bigger things, the kinds of things you come up with from reading *American Heritage,* history magazines, and newspaper articles that reference interesting turns of history, like the one about the discovery of George II's skull rattling around in a vault. The general knowledge I used on *Jeopardy!* came primarily from periodicals."

So after all this preparation, or, for many contestants, avoidance of same, what happens when they actually turn up at the studio?

GAME FACES

On taping day the contestants arrive at the studio at 10:30 A.M. and are met by our coordinators, who then accompany the thirteen prospective contestants until taping is complete. Security involving contestants is quite strict. They are allowed to associate only with each other and selected members of our staff. No one who has access to the game material has access to the contestants, for obvious reasons. Since we tape five shows in a day and cannot predict if one contestant will dominate the day's play, there is much waiting around, and the contestants have plenty of time to get to know one another, if they want to.

Paul Boymel remembers his fellow contestants as being "very, very friendly. There were a few people who were into heavy gamesmanship, but mostly there was a lot of camaraderie. Everybody knew that everybody there was good and there wasn't any point in trying to psych one another out. You did that when you played."

"It was really a great experience," enthuses Michael Rankins. "The contestant coordinators take real good care of the contestants, keeping everybody loose and comfortable. They made the backstage experience a lot less tension-filled than it could have been."

The all-time one-week money winner, Frank Spangenberg, remembers his fellow contestants fondly. "They were very agreeable, and we all got along. More than one person said to me, after I had won and they had lost, that they hoped I would go on and win it all. They were very nice."

And that's what we hope for when contestants play our game, a sense of fun and fellowship; being on *Jeopardy!* should be a kind of fantasy come to life, something to be savored rather than endured. But, clearly, there is a lot of money at stake, and that inescapable fact creates a certain level of tension in the participants. Over the years I've tried to remind contestants that it is not their own money at stake, it's "house" money, meant to be enjoyed. I recall the famous golfer Lee Trevino, known as one of the great pressure players of all time, answering a reporter's question about handling the heat when putting for hundreds of thousands of dollars on the pro tour. "Man, that ain't pressure," Trevino responded. "I'll take all the three-foot putts for fifty grand you want to give me. That's somebody else's money. Pressure is playing a guy for fifty bucks of your own money, when you only have a twenty in your pocket."

But as much as we advise our contestants to relax as best they can considering the circumstances, it can be a pressure cooker backstage, especially around tournament time. Our contestants want to win, and this desire sometimes manifests itself in the form of gamesmanship.

"There was always lots of psyching-out going on backstage," remembers Bob Rubin, who produced the show for eleven years. "Right from the beginning, some people took the show much more seriously than others."

"Some contestants actually asked one another trivia questions in the waiting room," remembers Eugene Finnerman. "People were trying to measure one another, or trying to create doubt in the other person's mind. During the tournament, one contestant tried to maintain a Zen composure, serious concentration. One player tried asserting the fact that he was a member of Mensa. And there was a lady who tried doing a Blanche Dubois imitation, worrying that she was going to make such a disgrace of herself on the air; of course she turned out to be one of the most aggressive players."

"Sure there was gamesmanship," states tournament participant Leah Greenwald, "and I thought it was fairly funny. Some people absolutely refused to talk to anyone. This possibly kept them calm, but I think they also wanted to avoid personal interactions with the other contestants so they could feel more comfortable being very competitive. There were a few of the quiz-kid type personalities who felt compelled to give a kind of compulsive knowledge display. I sat next to some of them in the audience during the final rounds of the tournament, and they could not prevent themselves from saying the answer. I'm not sure it was conscious gamesmanship; they were like the people in school who knew the answers to questions when nobody else in the classroom did and could not avoid saying them. The other people I was with were just ordinary people with lives and families, usually professional people of some sort. And what these two different general personality types have in common is a certain type of memory."

"I just think there is a lot of nervousness going on," champion Bob Verini observes, "and it can come out in a little bit of one-upsmanship. One of my opponents told me, between shows, that he and his wife had decided that if he won the hundred thousand dollars, they could have another baby. I don't think he was consciously trying to psych me out, because he was a very nice fellow. I just stayed within myself, read a magazine, and didn't talk much. But all the people in the tournament were nice."

And many contestants find that once they've appeared on *Jeopardy!* they become part of a unique fraternity. "After the tournament," Joel Sacks recalls, "you really have a sense of a shared experience. You have fifteen people from totally different backgrounds, but there is this common experience. Even contestants who didn't make it into the tournament return to watch the tapings; many of them came up to me and I could really relate to them, because they knew what I was going through."

Senior Tournament champion Zeke Sevilla of Virginia remains friendly with former competitors. "A lot of friendships came out of the show. We still hang around together, call one another every once in a while. One of them called the other day to say he was passing through town in a week, so we agreed to get together for dinner."

Michael Block won the Teen Tournament in 1988, and reports a convivial atmosphere backstage. "We sat around talking about girlfriends and sports and school. I think everyone was relaxed because it was Teen Tournaments, we're all kids. We played a trivia game where the person answering correctly got to ask the next question, and there was a little gamesmanship in that, because one kid kept asking outlandish literature questions, an obvious psych-out move. But it really wasn't bothering anybody." It particularly wasn't bothering Michael, who won the tournament and twenty-five thousand dollars.

"DON'T I KNOW YOU FROM SOMEWHERE?"

Jeopardy! contestants, particularly the champions, find that they not only make money and friends when appearing on the show but also find themselves dealing with what for all of them is a new phenomenon: fame.

"About six weeks after I'd won the tournament," says Mark Lowenthal, "I was down in Australia with my family. We're out on a catamaran in the Coral Sea, over the Great Barrier Reef, literally as far away from home as you can get without coming back the other way. And this American woman looks at me and says, 'You look very familiar,' and recognized me from the show. And I think that's quite remarkable.

"One day I was having lunch with Chuck Forrest in the executive dining room at the State Department, and we were discussing this issue of people stopping and talking to us about the show. We had a long talk about it. So after lunch we get in the elevator and another gentleman in there looks at both of us. By now we know the look. He said, 'I gotta ask you one question. What is Alex Trebek really like?' And Chuck and I just cracked up."

"Staten Island has a population of around four hundred thousand," says Michael Block, "and since the local paper really played up my win, everyone knew about it. I was getting telephone calls from people I didn't know, congratulating me. It got to the point where I couldn't move around too much. For a while it kind of got to me, because everyone wanted to be my friend. People would come up to me at school, and I had no idea who they were, but they put their arm around me and said, 'Hey, Mike, how ya doin' buddy?' But I was getting so much support from the community that I really appreciated it. Everyone's down on public education, especially in New York City—I went to Tottenville Public High School—and I'd like to say that it's great. Now I'm in an Ivy League college with people who went to Phillips, Horace Mann, Milton. But I don't care what they paid or what they say, I tell them my high school was the best. And since I was the *Jeopardy!* champ, they sort of listen to me . . .

"All the attention got to me a little bit, but my parents kept everything in perspective. They were very happy, very supportive the whole time. They're very education-oriented, and now every day that I'm in college I thank them for being that way. And I'm glad that when some parents are saying 'My son's a doctor' or 'My son's a lawyer,' my folks can say, 'My kid just won *Jeopardy!'* "

Architect Leah Greenwald knew that *Jeopardy!*'s ratings had to be quite high when she took her first walk after her shows aired. "I was walking down Massachusetts Avenue in Cambridge, and people stopped their cars and rolled down their windows to call out to me, saying 'Good work!' and things like that. I also got a number of telephone calls, including one from an eight-year-old boy who was a fan of the show."

Ouida Rellstab found out after her appearances on the show that she might have been operating with an unfair advantage. "I think all the nuns in New Orleans watch *Jeopardy!* I got many phone calls from nuns congratulating me, telling me they were praying for me to win (since I teach at St. Lawrence School). One of them even called up the local newspaper and reprimanded the editor for not having an article about me."

"It's been two years since I was originally on," says Roy Holliday, "and I'm still being stopped in the street. People will say I look familiar to them, and when I ask if they watch *Jeopardy!,* that does it. 'Yes, yes, I know you! You're the guy who got all the Southern Authors right. I remember you!' "

THE ENVELOPE, PLEASE

Nearly every *Jeopardy!* champion will tell you that being on the show is not about money. But, of course, the money can be nice. And since our champions are smart, they tend to be smart with their winnings, as well. A sampling:

Paul Boymel (attorney):   I was a private-practice attorney before I was on the show. After winning, I closed my office, went back to school for an advanced law degree, and got into a much more enjoyable type of work. I used my winnings to live on during that year of school.

Bob Verini (producer):   I started a theater company, the Manticore Theater, and we produce new plays and classics in New York City. *Jeopardy!* provided the seed money.

Frank Spangenberg: I'm a policeman. But with part of this money I'm going back to school for a master's. Perhaps law school in the future. But right now I'll be going for a master's in theology at St. John's University. It has nothing to do with work or anything practical, just something I want to do.

Leah Greenwald (architect):   I committed myself on the show to give some to my nephews and nieces, of whom I have eight, for educational purposes. And I did that. But I still had a chunk left over, and it's going into a new house. Since I just had triplets, this is very nice.

Michael Block (student):   Whatever the U.S. didn't take, U. Penn did.

Mark Lowenthal (political officer, State Department):   It's not like winning the lottery, which is *really* a lot of money. But it does give you certain financial opportunities.

Bruce Seymour: It's going to be my retirement fund; I've got it socked away in a bank. I have this aversion to gainful employment (so I have to save my money).

Eugene Finnerman (writer):   With the winnings, I decided to do the type of writing that I always wanted to. *Jeopardy!* has afforded me not only the gratification of fulfilling a dream but also about two years of freedom.

And *Jeopardy!*'s all-time money winner, Chuck Forrest? "I used it for law school. And the rest is just a cushion."

Royalty

JEOPARDY!

KINGS NAMED ED

Though never proven, it's believed little Edward V was smothered to death at this London location.

After Edward I killed the only native Welshman to hold this title, he gave it to his son.

In 1061 he was king of England; by 1161 he was a saint.

He was the oldest son of Queen Victoria.

The last Tudor king of England, he was the only surviving legitimate son of Henry VIII.

KINGS NAMED LOUIS

This great king of the Franks was succeeded in 814 by his son Louis the Debonair, aka the Pious.

In 1137 the future Louis VII married this fifteen-year-old heiress of Aquitaine.

Louis XIV was nicknamed "Le Roi Soleil," which means this.

Louis IX, who led Crusades to the Holy Land, was the only king of France to receive this honor.

Louis II of Bavaria, the notorious "Mad King Ludwig," was a fanatic admirer of this composer.

KINGS NAMED GEORGE

When not invited, George IV's wife tried to force her way into this ceremony in Westminster Abbey.

Legend says this king once shook hands with an oak tree, believing it was the King of Prussia.

The current Queen Mother was married to him, though she turned him down when he first proposed.

This son of Edward VII bore a striking resemblance to his cousin, Czar Nicholas II.

England's George I founded this British royal house.

ROYAL CATHERINES

Encyclopedia Americana says this Russian empress had ten lovers.

Of the six children of Catherine of Aragon and Henry VIII, only she lived to maturity.

When Henry VIII died, his widow, Catherine Parr, married Lord Seymour, brother of this queen.

Accused of affairs with her male secretary and her cousin, this fifth wife of Henry VIII was beheaded.

Three sons of Catherine de Medici became kings of this country, not Italy.

ROYAL ANNES

Anne of Brittany married two kings of this country, Charles VIII and Louis XII.

Reportedly, the ghosts of Elizabeth I and this woman, her mother, both haunt Windsor Castle.

Familial relationship of England's Queen Anne to the queen who preceded her, Mary II.

She's the royal mother of Peter and Zara Phillips.

This wife of Henry VIII was the daughter of a German duke.

ROYAL RUMORS

William II's death while hunting may have been murder; he died with one of these through his heart.

Some say Queen Victoria's grandson the Duke of Clarence was this notorious murderer.

This Egyptian reputedly used a mix of bear grease, horse's teeth, and burnt mice on her hair and eyelashes.

Her enemies said this second wife of Henry VIII had an extra finger on each hand.

She reportedly loves Mark Phillips, Coca-Cola, and horses, not necessarily in that order.

JEOPARDY!

KINGS NAMED ED	KINGS NAMED LOUIS	KINGS NAMED GEORGE
What was the Tower of London?	Who was Charlemagne?	What was his coronation?
What was Prince of Wales?	Who was Eleanor (of Aquitaine)?	Who was George III?
Who was Edward the Confessor? (DNA: Edward I)	What is the Sun King?	Who was George VI?
Who was Edward VII?	What is sainthood? (ACC: canonization)	Who was George V?
Who was Edward VI?	Who was Richard Wagner?	What was (the House of) Hanover?

ROYAL CATHERINES	ROYAL ANNES	ROYAL RUMORS
Who was Catherine the Great? (ACC: Catherine II)	What was France?	What is an arrow?
Who was Mary (I)? (ACC: Mary Tudor)	Who was Anne Boleyn?	Who was Jack the Ripper?
Who was Jane Seymour?	What was (younger) sister?	Who was Cleopatra?
Who was Catherine Howard?	Who is Princess Anne?	Who was Anne Boleyn?
What was France?	Who was Anne of Cleves?	Who is Princess Anne?

DOUBLE JEOPARDY!

TEEN QUEENS

This teenage Egyptian ruler gave birth to a son she claimed was Julius Caesar's.

Teen-aged Mary Queen of Scots also became queen of this country because she'd married the Dauphin.

At fifteen, she became the future Louis XVI's bride; at eighteen, she became queen.

British monarch crowned in 1837, when she was barely eighteen.

Many claim that before Bloody Mary grabbed the throne, this "Lady" was queen of England for nine days.

BRITISH SUCCESSION

Only son of George I.

Second son of George V, he was the current queen's father.

Henry IV was the last fourteenth-century king of England; this man was first to become king in the fifteenth century.

Henry VIII's father.

In Scotland, he was King James VI; in England, this first Stuart on the throne was called this.

THE ROYAL FAMILY

A Melanesian cult reportedly worships him, believing he secretly runs England behind his wife's back.

Prince Andrew gave Sarah Ferguson an engagement ring with this stone in it to match her hair.

Anna "Whiplash" Wallace spurned him, so he married the kid sister of another ex-girlfriend.

Though she married an ex-king, she was, ironically enough, barred from Windsor Castle.

In 1960 Queen Elizabeth II declared this the official surname of her children.

MORE ROYAL FAMILY

She was a nineteen-year-old kindergarten teacher when she became world-famous in 1981.

Prince Edward is his youngest child.

In 1985 he became the first heir to the British throne to begin his schooling outside the palace.

Prince Henry Charles Albert David, who was born in 1984, is known by this nickname.

The January 9, 1989, cover of *People* showed her in her helicopter pilot's helmet.

FRENCH ROYALTY

Isabella of France not only married this country's King Edward II, she helped depose him.

She inherited the Duchy of Aquitaine in 1137 and married the heir to the French throne the same year.

It was a mere hunting lodge before Louis XIV made it a dazzling royal residence.

Charles IX's mother induced him to order the St. Bartholomew's Day massacre of these people.

Voltaire said this stylish and influential mistress of Louis XV "loved the King for himself."

MOVIE ROYALTY

He played the King of France in *The Lion in Winter,* but now he's playing the king of spies, James Bond.

Paul Robeson played an African chieftain in the 1937 film about the search for this king's mines.

Flora Robson played this sixteenth-century queen twice, in *The Sea Hawk* and *Fire over England.*

This regal Russian role rated Janet Suzman a 1971 Oscar nomination.

Jose Ferrer made his movie debut as the Dauphin in this 1948 Ingrid Bergman film.

DOUBLE JEOPARDY!

TEEN QUEENS

Who was Cleopatra?

What was France?

Who was Marie Antoinette?

Who was Queen Victoria?

Who was Lady Jane Grey?

BRITISH SUCCESSION

Who was George II?

Who was George VI?

Who was Henry V?

Who was Henry VII?

What is James I?

THE ROYAL FAMILY

Who is Prince Philip?
(ACC: Duke of Edinburgh)

What is a ruby?

Who is Prince Charles?
(ACC: Prince of Wales)

Who is the Duchess of Windsor?
(ACC: Wallis Warfield Simpson)

What is Mountbatten-Windsor?

MORE ROYAL FAMILY	FRENCH ROYALTY	MOVIE ROYALTY
Who is Princess Diana? (ACC: Lady Diana Spencer, Princess of Wales)	What is England?	Who is Timothy Dalton?
Who is Prince Philip? (ACC: The Duke of Edinburgh)	Who was Eleanor of Aquitaine?	Who was King Solomon?
Who is (Prince) William (of Wales)?	What is Versailles?	Who was Elizabeth I?
What is Harry?	What were the Huguenots? (ACC: Protestants)	What was Empress Alexandra?
Who is Fergie, the Duchess of York?	Who was Madame de Pompadour?	What was *Joan of Arc?*

FINAL JEOPARDY!

CATEGORY: RULERS

The only name shared by four consecutive kings of England.

FINAL JEOPARDY!

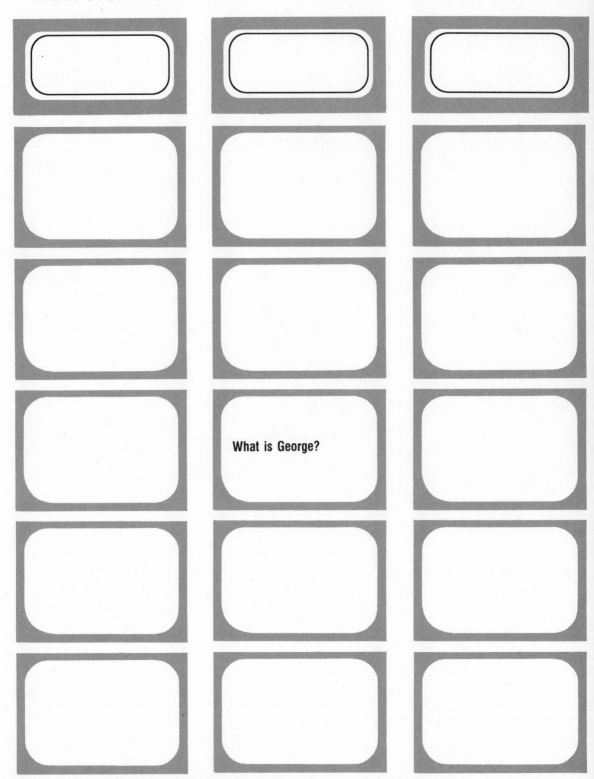

What is George?

The Champs

When you survey *Jeopardy!* contestants, fans, producers, and staff on the subject of the best players ever seen on the show, two names continually emerge: Burns Cameron from the original show and Chuck Forrest from the new show. Burns won the tournament in 1966 ($11,110), and Chuck in 1986 ($172,800). Both of them won in runaways. Herewith, a few comments from each.

BURNS CAMERON

STRATEGY: I remember the fun I had. I approached it as a game, and never really thought about the money until Final Jeopardy! You want to be relaxed, but not so relaxed that you lose your edge. During one of my games, I was competing against two women who combated their nerves by having several martinis prior to the show. They not only couldn't come up with the answers, they also couldn't even locate the buzzer. I got so far ahead that I slowed down just to help them.

PREPARATION: Not really much you can do. Know the states and capitals, that kind of thing.

HIS STRENGTH: My ability to read quickly and know instantly when I could answer. Since in those days we could ring in upon exposure of the material, my advantage was I just read faster than everyone else.

TODAY'S *Jeopardy!*:   Some of the material is harder, some easier than the old days. But I think it is harder to win now, since you can't ring in until Alex finishes reading the answer. That gives all contestants a chance to think and catch up with the quick players. I'd be interested in trying my luck in the new version.

CHUCK FORREST

CONTESTANT TEST: It's pretty hard, because the time allotted to take it is short.

STRATEGY: Don't get a lot of them wrong. It's a double whammy if you guess wrong and an opponent gets it right. Back off when you're not sure. I bounced around the board. That throws people off because you know where you're going, where to look on the board, and the other players can't move their heads to keep up with you. I kept track of the money so that I knew where I stood during the game. I was conservative with Daily Doubles, and in Final Jeopardy! I always had more than twice the amount of my opponents, so I didn't have to worry about strategy there.

PREPARATION: I played the home version of the game, and practiced buzzing in when I watched the show. Reading trivia books is a waste of time. I memorized all the Oscar winners, and that never came up.

GAMESMANSHIP: It was mostly friendly backstage. One contestant did try to psych me out, and admitted as much. It bothered me, but I didn't let him think that it did.

HIS ABILITY: *Jeopardy!* is a form of remembering things. A lot of people know the answers but can't come up with them quickly. It has to do with the way your mind is arranged.

CURRENT OCCUPATION: I'm a political officer for the State Department, stationed in Dubai, United Arab Emirates. I've always been fascinated by Middle Eastern affairs.

FAME: I get recognized back home in Michigan, and even in Saudi Arabia, because *Jeopardy!* plays on armed forces television. Everyone asks me the same three things: (1) Will I ever be back on the show? (I'm hoping for a Super Tournament someday.) (2) What's Alex like? (Nice guy.) (3) Did I have to pay taxes on my winnings? (Of course.)

Tournament of Champions #1

JEOPARDY!

ASIAN HISTORY

Talks were held during October 1951 in Panmunjom to reunify this country, but they didn't work.

In 1972, this country returned control of Okinawa to Japan.

Estimated death toll from famous 1756 incident in this room in an Indian fort ranges from fifteen to more than one hundred.

A former monk turned rebellious, then merciless, founded this Chinese dynasty in 1368.

It was completed during World War I and linked eastern and western Siberia.

SCIENCE

Joseph Priestley developed this process without which there would be no Coke, no Pepsi.

French aristocrat Antoine Lavoisier burned diamonds to prove they are made of this substance.

After about eight weeks a human embryo develops into this.

At about 63,000 ft. at normal body temperature, blood will do this.

Because they are never found in chemical compounds, the noble gases neon, argon, and helium are called this.

FOOD

The Quechua language of Peru has about one thousand words for these tubers Peruvians have grown for eight thousand years.

Of yogurt, liver, or tofu, the food Americans hate most, according to *Harper's Index*.

This hard-shelled high-calorie nut, native to Australia, is also called the Queensland nut.

Larousse says kasha is the Russian word for this cooked grain.

Coral, an edible greenish substance that turns pink when cooked, is found in the ovaries of this animal.

PRESIDENTIAL LIFE SPANS

February 12, 1809–April 15, 1865.

April 13, 1743–July 4, 1826.

October 30, 1735–July 4, 1826.

May 8, 1884–December 26, 1972.

August 10, 1874–October 20, 1964.

GEOGRAPHICAL SONGS

"Hooray for" this city, where you're terrific if you're even good.

"If God didn't make little green apples, then it don't rain" here "in the summertime."

"Me and Mamie O'Rourke, tripped the light fantastic on" these.

Cole Porter wrote that this city "loves lovers, for lovers it's heaven above."

"Ragtime Cowboy Joe" was a "high-falutin' scootin', shootin' son-of-a-gun from" this state.

"OLD" AND "NEW"

A semiaquatic salamander.

If a pregnant woman eats strawberries, her baby will have a strawberry-shaped birthmark, for example.

Tom Cruise sang this song in "Risky Business"; Ron Reagan sang it on "Saturday Night Live."

The only independent country in the world that fits this category.

Annual award given by the American Library Association for the outstanding American children's book.

JEOPARDY!

ASIAN HISTORY	SCIENCE	FOOD
What is Korea?	What is carbonating water?	What are potatoes?
What is the United States?	What is carbon?	What is tofu?
What is the Black Hole of Calcutta? (ACC: Ft. William storeroom)	What is a fetus?	What is the macadamia?
What is the Ming Dynasty? (ACC: Hung-Wu)	What is boil?	What is buckwheat?
What is the Trans-Siberian Railroad?	What is inert?	What is a lobster?

PRESIDENTIAL LIFE SPANS	GEOGRAPHICAL SONGS	"OLD" AND "NEW"
Who was Abe Lincoln?	What is Hollywood?	What is a newt?
Who was Thomas Jefferson?	What is Indianapolis?	What is an old wives' tale?
Who was John Adams?	What were "The Sidewalks of New York"?	What is "Old Time Rock and Roll"?
Who was Harry Truman?	What is Paris?	What is New Zealand? (ACC: Papua New Guinea)
Who was Herbert Hoover?	What is Arizona?	What is the Newbery Medal?

DOUBLE JEOPARDY!

AVIATION

On October 1, 1986, Northwest Airlines took this word out of its name.

To serve as Air Force One, two of this model are currently on order from Boeing.

One of the two biggest makers of commercial jet aircraft engines in the United States.

Its acquisition of People Express, Frontier, Continental, and Eastern have made it the biggest U.S. air company.

Some claim that the Wright brothers made only a power glider and that this Brazilian really invented the airplane.

IDAHOANS

Encyclopedia Americana says this guide of Lewis and Clark lived to about one hundred while the *Britannica* says she died at twenty-six.

Idaho's highest point, Borah Peak, is named for William E. Borah, who held this office for thirty-three years.

It's where you'd go to see Idaho-born sculptor Gutzon Borglum's most famous work.

"The poet's poet," his writings were far more influential than his World War II broadcasts from fascist Italy.

This former Bendix executive and his wife, Mary Cunningham, now run their own venture capital firm.

THE CIVIL WAR

It wasn't until the May 1864 Battle of the Wilderness that these two generals encountered each other.

In 1861, this Texas governor was deposed for refusing to support secession.

Warship that was called "The Cheesebox on a Raft."

Julia Ward Howe wrote "The Battle Hymn of the Republic" to be sung to the tune of this song.

This abolitionist congressman from Pennsylvania insisted on being buried in an integrated cemetery.

SHAVIAN CHARACTERS

In Shaw's play about her, this Russian empress rhapsodizes about Voltaire, who historically was her pen pal.

Performances of "Mrs. Warren's Profession" were banned because this was Mrs. Warren's profession.

Heroine who says, "My voices have deceived me . . . but only a fool will walk into a fire."

This play has characters named Snobby Price, Rummy Mitchens, and Barbara Undershaft.

Of all his characters, Captain Shotover of this title domicile may be the most like Shaw himself.

ODD ALPHABETS

In alphabet radio code, "B" is Bravo and "F" shares its name with this dance.

Edible letters produced by Post.

In ASCII, this kind of computer code, *A* is 01000001.

In the sign-language alphabet, it's the first letter whose sign resembles it.

Representing the sound of the *a* in *about,* a small *e* turned upside down is called this.

POTPOURRI

In October 1986, the U.S. mint issued the first of these in more than fifty years.

Iva D'Aguino, who in 1977 received a presidential pardon, was better known by this nickname.

Guinness says the greatest number of people saved by one man from death were saved by him in 1944–45.

He won a lifetime membership in the U.S. Duffers Association after missing the first golf ball he swung at on the moon.

Once denied a driver's license, this general secretary of the U.S. Communist party is usually driven to work.

DOUBLE JEOPARDY!

AVIATION	IDAHOANS	THE CIVIL WAR
What is Orient?	Who was Sacajawea? (ACC: Bird Woman)	Who were Grant and Lee?
What is a 747?	What is U.S. senator?	Who was Sam Houston?
What are Pratt and Whitney (United Technologies) or G.E.?	What is Mount Rushmore (South Dakota)?	What was the *Monitor?*
What is Texas Air?	Who was Ezra Pound?	What is "John Brown's Body"?
Who was Albert (O.) Santos-Dumont?	Who is William Agee?	Who was Thaddeus Stevens?

SHAVIAN CHARACTERS	ODD ALPHABETS	POTPOURRI
Who was Catherine the Great? (ACC: Catherine II or "Great Catherine")	What is the foxtrot?	What is gold coin?
What was prostitution? (ACC: a madam)	What are Alpha-Bits?	Who was Tokyo Rose?
Who is St. Joan?	What is binary code?	Who is Raoul Wallenberg?
What is *Major Barbara*?	What is *C?*	Who is Alan Shepard?
What is *Heartbreak House*?	What is a schwa?	Who is Gus Hall?

FINAL JEOPARDY!

CATEGORY: NINETEENTH-CENTURY DEMOCRATS

He said, "I am the last President of the United States."

FINAL JEOPARDY!

Who was
James Buchanan?

How to Become
a *Jeopardy!* Contestant

Ever watch the show with the certainty that you could do just as well as the contestants playing on television? Here's how you go about finding out.

The regular show is open to anyone eighteen years of age or older who passes our contestant screening exam and interview. (The Teen and College Tournament contestants are selected from special searches.) However, passing the tests does not *guarantee* you will actually be picked as a contestant. Even being invited to the studio for a taping does not carry an absolute guarantee you will be on the show. On taping days we cannot predict how many games a particular champion will win, so we can never know exactly how many contestants will be necessary to complete the five shows (we tape ten shows over a two-day period).

Step One is to take the written exam.

Our contestant coordinators travel the country on a regular basis, administering the exam. Prior to our arrival in a city, the local station that airs *Jeopardy!* will run a newspaper announcement and broadcast special promos. We encourage people to write rather than call when we are on an out-of-town search because the announcement elicits an avalanche of respondents and the stations' telephone operators are not equipped for the overload.

Sending in a card, however, doesn't guarantee that you'll be able to take the test at one of our out-of-town tryouts. In large cities, like New York or Vancouver, we sometimes receive 100,000 cards, and our coordinators can handle only five hundred contestants during the visit. So the cards are chosen at random, and the "winners" are given appointments.

The tests consist of fifty general-knowledge questions, and they are definitely challenging. We've printed examples of the tests in this book to give you an idea of what to expect. They are graded immediately, and the people who pass are invited to play a mock version of the game.

If you do well on the test and playing the game, we keep your telephone number and call you when and if we have an opening. It can be as soon as a couple of weeks or as long as a year. Or not at all. Such are the vagaries of game shows.

Don't be shy about taking the test just because you didn't graduate Phi Beta Kappa from an Ivy League university. *Jeopardy!* is a general-knowledge game and there is no formula for who or what makes a great player.

To take the test at our offices, you can call (213) 466-3931 to schedule an appointment. The test is given on a regular basis. Remember, however, that if you are selected to appear on the show, you must travel to Los Angeles at your own expense, win or lose, and all costs incurred during your stay are yours alone. Any costs involved with your traveling to take our screening tests are your responsibility as well.

Given the above, we'd love to have you on *Jeopardy!,* so don't be shy, give it a try.

Teen Contestant Exam #1*

1. THE FIFTIES
   In 1958, France, West Germany, Italy, Belgium, the Netherlands, and Luxembourg formed this.
2. ROARING TWENTIES
   After his 1927 flight to Paris, he was given a ticker-tape parade in New York.
3. AMERICAN HISTORY
   He led the first European expedition to what is now Florida.
4. ANCIENT HISTORY
   This conqueror died June 13, 323 B.C., at Babylon.

*Applicants are allotted only ten seconds to answer each question.

5. U.S. HISTORY
Warren Berger swore her in, September 25, 1981.

6. SPACE AND AVIATION
On May 5, 1961, he became the first American to go into space.

7. THE HUMAN BODY
The lingual nerve carries sensations from this muscle to the brain.

8. SCIENCE
When bread is "leavened," this gas is responsible for the expansion of the dough.

9. THE SOLAR SYSTEM
Its four largest moons are referred to collectively as the Galilean moons.

10. ZOOLOGY
The vicuna is native to these mountains.

11. LITERATURE
County in which Twain's "Jumping Frog" jumped.

12. PEN NAMES
Reverend Charles Dodgson's pen name.

13. COMPOSERS
He wrote more than a thousand works but left one symphony "unfinished."

14. BALLET
In ballet, number of basic positions of the feet.

15. ARTISTS
Century during which Vincent Van Gogh did his painting.

16. THE BIBLE
In the fight with David, Goliath represented these people.

17. MYTHOLOGY
The Greek goddess of love.

18. THE 50 STATES
State bordered by the greatest number of Great Lakes.

19. GEOGRAPHY
Though this country has more than seven thousand islands, half the population lives on one—Luzon.

20. BODIES OF WATER
The Danube empties into this body of water.

21. FOOD
In the 1840s, Ephraim Bull developed a variety of grapes in this Massachusetts town.

22. HOLIDAYS AND OBSERVANCES
In this state, the last Monday in March is Seward's Day.

23. POLITICIANS
Jane Byrne was this city's first woman mayor.

24. WORLD LEADERS
In 1985, Mikhail Gorbachev succeeded this man as top Soviet leader.

25. TRAVEL AND TOURISM
You can visit the skydeck on the 103rd floor of this, the tallest building in the U.S.

26. INVENTORS
On June 21, 1834, he received a patent for his mechanical reaper.

27. MONEY
Ninety-nine percent of paper currency circulating in the U.S. was issued by this body.

28. CIVICS
By the 1982 deadline, only thirty-five states had ratified this amendment though thirty-eight were needed.

29. JEWELRY
The sacred Egyptian beetle often represented in jewelry.

30. DENTISTRY
This thin bacteria-laden layer that forms on the teeth can harden into tartar.

31. ENGINEERING
The huge man-made wonder on the Colorado River completed in 1936.

32. AWARDS
Awards established by a newspaper publisher, now given out by Columbia University.

33. ANTHROPOLOGY
These people, who call themselves "Inuit," occupy parts of Greenland, the USSR, and the U.S.

34. ARTS AND CRAFTS
Old English for a drying house, it's where potters put their pots to bake.

35. BUSINESS
C. A. Thomas, Isaac Pitman, and J. R. Gregg each developed a system of this.

36. SPORTS
In 1976, she became the last American to win a gold medal in ladies' figure skating at the Winter Olympics.

37. SPORTS HISTORY
The Marquess of Queensbury developed the modern rules of this sport.

38. SUPERHEROES
Before his bio was revised, Superman was reported to have grown up in this town.

39. MOVIE BROTHERS
John Candy played Tom Hanks's brother in this 1984 romantic comedy.

40. THE SIXTIES
The tales of P. L. Travers were translated to the screen for this 1964 musical about a nanny.

41. NURSERY RHYMES
"Diddle diddle dumpling, my son John, went to bed with" these on.

42. LEAD SINGERS
David Byrne is the lead singer for this group.

43. ROCK ALBUMS
His albums include *Face Value, Hello, I Must Be Going!,* and *No Jacket Required.*

44. TV ROLES
Role played by Loretta Swit, Meg Foster, and Sharon Gless.

45. BROADWAY
Musical which features the song "There Is Nothing Like a Dame."

46. FOREIGN PHRASES
English translation of *requiescat in pace,* usually found etched in marble.

47. NINE-LETTER WORDS
The skin of a sheep or goat prepared to be written on.

48. FAMOUS QUOTES
Poe wrote of "The glory that was Greece" and this "that was Rome."

49. DEFINITIONS
From the Greek, *osteo* is a prefix meaning this.

50. STARTS WITH X
This inert gas is the only chemical element to begin with *x*.

1. Common Market/EEC
2. Charles Lindbergh
3. Ponce de Leon
4. Alexander the Great

5. Sandra Day O'Connor
6. Alan B. Shepard
7. Tongue
8. Carbon dioxide/CO_2
9. Jupiter
10. The Andes
11. Calaveras
12. Lewis Carroll
13. Schubert
14. Five
15. Nineteenth/1800s
16. Philistines
17. Aphrodite
18. Michigan
19. The Philippines
20. The Black Sea
21. Concord
22. Alaska
23. Chicago
24. (Konstantin) Chernenko
25. Sears Tower
26. Cyrus McCormick
27. Federal Reserve
28. ERA (Equal Rights Amendment)

29. Scarab
30. Plaque
31. Boulder Dam (Hoover Dam)
32. Pulitzer Prizes
33. Eskimos
34. Kiln
35. Shorthand
36. Dorothy Hamill
37. Boxing
38. Smallville
39. *Splash*
40. *Mary Poppins*
41. His stockings (ACC: stocking and one shoe)
42. Talking Heads
43. Phil Collins
44. (Chris/Christine) Cagney
45. *South Pacific*
46. Rest in peace
47. Parchment
48. (The) grandeur
49. Bone
50. Xenon

Teen Contestant Exam #2

1. U.S. HISTORY
   In March 1785, this future president succeeded Ben Franklin as minister to France.

2. EXPLORERS
   He introduced potatoes to Ireland and gave Virginia its name.

3. RULERS
   Family name of Russia's last czar, Nicholas II.

4. PRESIDENTIAL TRIVIA
   Seven U.S. presidents, including Hayes and Taft, were born in this state.

5. HISTORY
   Founded a year after Jamestown, it's the oldest city in Canada.

6. ASIAN HISTORY

Empire that controlled most of Asia and Eastern Europe in the late thirteenth century.

7. MATHEMATICS

Base-2 number equivalent to the base-10 number 3.

8. PREHISTORIC TIMES

The name of this extinct animal means three-horned face.

9. ANIMALS

The kangaroo is the largest animal of this order.

10. SCIENCE

Pumice is a spongelike solid formed on top of this substance.

11. CHEMISTRY

While H_2O is water, H_2O_2 is this.

12. SHAKESPEARE

This king was Cordelia's father.

13. LITERATURE

Jack London tale in which the main character, Buck, becomes leader of the pack.

14. OPERA

Rossini's last opera, it tells the story of a national hero.

15. ART

Artist who painted *Arrangement in Grey and Black, No. 1: The Artist's Mother.*

16. OLD TESTAMENT

Name of the person God told Abraham to sacrifice.

17. MYTHOLOGY

Athena turned Arachne into one of these creatures.

18. RIVERS AND LAKES

These two colorful Nile rivers merge at Khartoum, Sudan.

19. GEOGRAPHY

Sri Lanka lies about twenty miles off the coast of this country.

20. WORLD CAPITALS

Karachi and Rawalpindi have both been capitals of this country.

21. INTERNATIONAL CUISINE

The two ingredients in this Hawaiian dish are taro and water.

22. HOLIDAYS

Groundhog Day is observed on this date.

23. MONARCHS

In 1301, Edward I gave this title to his oldest son who was born at Caernarvon Castle.

24. IN THE NEWS

In 1986, he became the first black archbishop of Cape Town, South Africa.

25. TRAVEL AND TOURISM

One-word name for the temple whose ruins stand atop Athens's Acropolis Hill.

26. INVENTIONS

In 1915, to conduct the first ever transcontinental phone call, Alexander Graham Bell once again called this man.

27. MONEY

There are U.S. mints making coins in San Francisco, Denver, and this city.

28. CONGRESS

Standing, select, conference, and joint are the four types of these.

29. SIGNS AND SYMBOLS

Each time a person takes this office, a new fisherman's ring is made.

30. MEDICINE

Iodine is added to table salt to help prevent this glandular deficiency disorder.

31. POLITICS

Term for an office-holder soon to leave office, usually due to defeat for reelection.

32. MAGAZINES

Some of the magazines published in this city are *The New Republic* and *National Geographic*.

33. SOCIAL SCIENCES

Trained as a neurologist, he developed psychoanalysis.

34. PRINTING

Movable type was invented in this country circa A.D. 1045.

35. MUSICAL INSTRUMENTS

When divided into three major groups, instruments are classed as stringed, wind, and these.

36. THE OLYMPICS

The 1984 U.S. gold medalist coached by Romanian Bela Karolyi.

37. STADIUMS

It was the world's first indoor baseball and football stadium.

38. SUPERHEROES

Wonder Woman used these accessories to deflect bullets.

39. ACTORS AND ROLES

Nickname of Tom Cruise's character in *Top Gun,* or last name of a James Garner TV character.

40. DISNEY MOVIES
Bambi's friend Flower was one of these animals.
41. NURSERY RHYMES
"When the boys came out to play," he "ran away."
42. POP MUSIC
Rock group with Terri Nunn on vocals.
43. RECORDING ARTISTS
Since leaving Genesis, he's released *So* and four albums with his own name for titles.
44. TELEVISION
From 1978–1986 he played Arnold Jackson.
45. MUSICALS
Professor Harold Hill is the title character of this musical set in the Midwest.
46. PROVERBS
It's "the soul of wit."
47. FRENCH PHRASES
The "Rive Gauche" of the Seine is this.
48. STARTS WITH *CRU*
Water fleas and barnacles are types of these.
49. QUOTES
In 1917 Woodrow Wilson said, "The world must be made safe for" this.
50. INITIALS
The initials *RAF* stand for this, as Winston Churchill could have told you.

1. Thomas Jefferson
2. Sir Walter Raleigh
3. Romanoff
4. Ohio
5. Quebec
6. Mongol Empire
7. 11
8. Triceratops
9. Marsupials
10. Lava
11. Hydrogen Peroxide
12. King Lear
13. *Call of the Wild*
14. *William Tell*
15. James (Abbott McNeill) Whistler
16. Isaac
17. Spider
18. Blue and White
19. India
20. Pakistan
21. Poi
22. February 2
23. Prince of Wales
24. (Desmond) Tutu
25. Parthenon
26. (Dr. Thomas A.) Watson
27. Philadelphia
28. Committees

29. Pope
30. Goiter
31. Lame duck
32. Washington, D.C.
33. Sigmund Freud
34. China
35. Percussion
36. Mary Lou Retton
37. Astrodome (Harris County Domed Stadium)
38. (Golden) bracelets
39. Maverick

40. Skunk
41. Georgie Porgie
42. Berlin
43. Peter Gabriel
44. Gary Coleman
45. *The Music Man*
46. Brevity
47. Left Bank
48. Crustaceans
49. Democracy
50. Royal Air Force

Adult Contestant Exam #1

1. 1955
    In December 1955, Martin Luther King, Jr., led a boycott of this city's bus system.
2. WORLD HISTORY
    Secessionist state that fought unsuccessfully for its independence from Nigeria in the late 1960s.
3. PRESIDENTS
    In a space of seventeen days, this president escaped two assassination attempts.
4. THE RENAISSANCE
    Cardinal Thomas Wolsey was a favorite chancellor of this king.
5. ANCIENT TIMES
    He reportedly walked the streets of Athens looking for an honest man.
6. WORLD CAPITALS
    The capital of Burma.
7. SOUTH AMERICA
    Formerly Dutch Guiana, it's now called this.
8. DOGS
    Once used to save drowning sailors, this breed was named for the Canadian province in which it was developed.
9. ARCHITECTURE
    He built London's St. Paul's Cathedral and is buried there.

10. SHAKESPEAREAN CHARACTERS
In *A Midsummer Night's Dream,* she's the Queen of the Fairies.
11. POETRY
Poet whose middle name was Bysshe.
12. WOMEN AUTHORS
This Alice Walker novel was a best seller in 1982.
13. OPERA
He wrote *Lohengrin.*
14. CLASSICAL MUSIC
His best-known concertos are called "The Four Seasons."
15. RELIGIOUS HISTORY
His translation of the Bible into German is considered a literary masterpiece.
16. CHEMISTRY
On the Fahrenheit scale, number of degrees between the freezing and boiling points of water.
17. ASTRONOMY
First seen in 1973, this comet will be seen again in 75,000 years.
18. BUSINESS AND INDUSTRY
The Royal Dutch Petroleum Company is a parent of this oil company.
19. CONGRESS
From Dutch for "free booter," it's a delaying tactic first used in the nineteenth century.
20. GOVERNMENT
Plans submitted by Ben Franklin became the basis of this, the first U.S. "Constitution."
21. RELIGION
This religion's sacred writings are the Vedas.
22. FASHION DESIGNERS
Her symbol is a swan.
23. FOOD AND DRINK
"Baked Alaska" is ice cream covered with this right before baking.
24. ANATOMY
The integumentary system consists of the hair, nails, and this.
25. COLLEGE MASCOTS
The U.S. Naval Academy uses one of these animals as a mascot.
26. PUBLISHERS
He stated the premise of *Life* magazine as "people like to look at pictures."

27. COLORS
The number of spectral colors in a rainbow.

28. HOLIDAYS AND OBSERVANCES
Until June 1, 1954, Veterans Day was called this in the United States.

29. MYTHOLOGY
The Oracle in this Greek city was considered to be the center of the world.

30. AWARDS
A Pulitzer Prize in history is awarded for a work on the history of this.

31. MIDDLE AGES
Flag use became widespread with increased interest in this, the study of family crests.

32. ECONOMICS
Noted economist and ambassador to India under JFK.

33. LANGUAGES
This country's four official languages are Italian, German, French, and Romansh.

34. FAMOUS TRIALS
His jury of 501 men found him guilty of corrupting the youth of Athens.

35. FAMOUS COUPLES
Late choreographer who was once married to Gwen Verdon.

36. SINGERS
Legend says this "Swedish Nightingale" gave concerts in Kentucky's Mammoth Cave.

37. SPORTSCASTERS
Miss America 1971, she became a pioneer woman sportscaster on *The NFL Today.*

38. BALLET
European capital in which Diaghilev founded the Ballets Russes.

39. KIDDY LIT
Kipling's Rikki-Tikki-Tavi was one of these animals.

40. WOMEN IN SPORTS
The first time in thirteen years that this tennis player didn't win a Grand Slam event was 1987.

41. NICKNAMES
John Barrymore's "facial" nickname.

42. ACTORS AND ROLES
Chief Thundercloud, Jay Silverheels, and Michael Horse all played this famous Indian.

43. DOUBLE DOUBLE LETTERS
A cuspidor.

44. WORD PLAY
State whose two-letter postal abbreviation is a homophone of an antonym of full.

45. "PROS" AND "CONS"
Surrounding food with dry, hot, circulated air, it's a type of oven.

46. WORDS
From the Latin meaning "for all," it can be an anthology or a mode of public transportation.

47. ACRONYMS
It's what the *E* in *OPEC* stands for.

48. ALPHABETS
The last letter of the Greek alphabet.

49. NUMERICAL PHRASES
Once the highest order of Freemasonry, it now refers to relentless questioning.

50. GRAMMAR
An adverb can modify a verb, another adverb, or this part of speech.

1. Montgomery
2. Biafra
3. Gerald Ford
4. Henry VIII
5. Diogenes
6. Rangoon
7. Surinam(e)
8. Newfoundland
9. Christopher Wren
10. Titania
11. (Percy) Shelley
12. *The Color Purple*
13. Richard Wagner
14. Antonio Vivaldi
15. Martin Luther
16. 180
17. Kohoutek
18. Shell
19. Filibuster
20. The Articles of Confederation
21. Hinduism
22. Gloria Vanderbilt
23. Meringue
24. Skin
25. Goat
26. Henry Luce
27. Seven
28. Armistice Day
29. Delphi
30. The United States
31. Heraldry
32. John Kenneth Galbraith
33. Switzerland
34. Socrates

35. Bob Fosse
36. Jenny Lind
37. Phyllis George
38. Paris
39. Mongoose
40. Chris Evert (Lloyd)
41. "The Great Profile"
42. Tonto

43. Spittoon
44. Montana (MT)
45. Convection
46. Omnibus
47. Exporting
48. Omega
49. The Third Degree
50. Adjective

Adult Contestant Exam #2

1. **RECENT HISTORY**
   In 1964, Congress passed this resolution which gave LBJ power to "take all necessary measures."

2. **THE TWENTIETH CENTURY**
   Antonio Salazar was a leader of this country.

3. **EIGHTEENTH-CENTURY AMERICA**
   In 1779, Richmond replaced this city as Virginia's capital.

4. **POLITICIANS**
   In 1979, he resigned as U.S. Ambassador to the U.N. but was later elected mayor of Atlanta.

5. **FAMOUS AMERICANS**
   Technically, this lawyer lost the 1925 Scopes "monkey" trial.

6. **GEOGRAPHY**
   The Jutland Peninsula juts out from this European country.

7. **WORLD GEOGRAPHY**
   It's bordered by the Netherlands, West Germany, Luxembourg, France, and the North Sea.

8. **ANIMALS**
   North America's most common species of pigeon, it was named for its sad cooing notes.

9. **SCULPTURE**
   This broken statue was found on, and partially named for, the island of Melos.

10. **SHAKESPEARE**
    Character who said, "All the perfumes of Arabia will not sweeten this little hand."

11. POETRY
A Japanese poem of seventeen syllables.

12. LITERATURE
Southern author of *Sanctuary* and its sequel, *Requiem for a Nun*.

13. OPERA
Carmen is set in this city in Spain.

14. CLASSICAL MUSIC
He composed the famous *Minute Waltz*.

15. THE BIBLE
King Solomon's mother.

16. THE SOLAR SYSTEM
One of its moons, Io, has active volcanoes.

17. MATHEMATICS
An angle exceeding 90 degrees but less than 180.

18. CHEMISTRY
Niels Bohr's model explained the structure of this.

19. BUSINESS AND INDUSTRY
It's what the *A* stands for in *GMAC*.

20. LAW
From Latin for "command," it's a court order stopping a person from doing something.

21. THE CABINET
In 1947, James Forrestal became the first secretary of this cabinet department.

22. RELIGIOUS LEADERS
As the founder of the Salvation Army, he became a general.

23. FASHION DESIGNERS
Born in 1883, she was famous for designing simple tailored suits worn with ropes of pearls.

24. FOOD
This fruit is also called an alligator pear.

25. ANATOMY
When you swallow, it's the tube into which the food goes first.

26. EUROPE
The Spanish Riding School, known for training lipizzaners, is in this city.

27. HERBS AND SPICES
Also called "deadly nightshade," its name is Italian for "fair lady."

28. ORGANIZATIONS
This volunteer youth patrol is famous for wearing red berets.

29. HOLIDAYS AND OBSERVANCES
New Year's Day and this are the two Federal holidays that can fall on the first of the month.

30. MYTHOLOGY
Aphrodite's love, his name is synonymous with masculine beauty.

31. AWARDS
Named for Antoinette Perry, these awards have been given annually since 1947.

32. FLAGS
The U.N. flag has a map of the world surrounded by two of these.

33. ECONOMICS
His *Inquiry into the Nature and Causes of the Wealth of Nations* was written in 1776.

34. LANGUAGES
This dead language was the basic language of ancient India.

35. PHILOSOPHERS
He listed seven sages of ancient Greece, but his teacher, Socrates, was not among them.

36. DANCERS
One-word nickname of tap dancer Bill Robinson.

37. BESTSELLERS
Loon Lake and *Ragtime* are among his bestsellers.

38. THE FUNNIES
His off-beat humor is featured in "The Far Side."

39. MOVIE TOUGH GUYS
In a classic movie scene, he shoved a grapefruit in Mae Clarke's face.

40. ACTRESSES
Glenda Jackson's most famous role on *Masterpiece Theatre.*

41. FAIRY TALES
"Le Chat Botte" is the French title of this fairy tale.

42. SPORTS
Floyd Patterson became first man to regain the heavyweight championship when he K.O.'d this Swede June 20, 1960.

43. OLD RADIO
As Professor Le Blanc, Mel Blanc played his "violin teacher."

44. NAMES
This name of the wife of Odysseus, who waited twenty years for his return, has come to mean a faithful wife.

45. STARTS WITH *G*
In the British army, it's a soldier from Nepal.

46. METALLIC PHRASES
It describes the proverb based on Luke 6:31.

47. NUMBER, PLEASE
Total zeros in one quadrillion.

48. LETTER PERFECT
Single-letter abbreviation that indicates 1,000 in the metric system.

49. NUMBER, PLEASE
You'll often find this number preceding "-square," "-bagger," and "-flusher."

50. GRAMMAR
In "The quick red fox jumped over the lazy brown dog," this word is the object of the preposition.

1. Tonkin Gulf
2. Portugal
3. Williamsburg
4. Andrew Young
5. Clarence Darrow
6. Denmark
7. Belgium
8. Mourning Dove
9. Venus de Milo
10. Lady Macbeth
11. Haiku
12. William Faulkner
13. Seville
14. Frederic Chopin
15. Bathsheba
16. Jupiter
17. Obtuse
18. Atom
19. Acceptance
20. Injunction
21. Department of Defense
22. William Booth
23. (Gabrielle) (Coco) Chanel
24. Avocado
25. Esophagus
26. Vienna
27. Belladonna
28. Guardian Angels
29. Labor Day
30. Adonis
31. Tony
32. Olive Branches
33. Adam Smith
34. Sanskrit
35. Plato
36. Bojangles
37. E. L. Doctorow
38. Gary Larson
39. Jimmy Cagney
40. Elizabeth (R)
41. Puss in Boots
42. Ingemar Johansson
43. Jack Benny
44. Penelope
45. Gurkha
46. The Golden Rule
47. 15 (Fifteen)
48. K
49. Four (4)
50. Dog

Of Mice and Women

JEOPARDY!

MICKEY MOUSE

In 1933 Walt Disney said that Mickey was married to this costar in real life.

First it was Walt; then it was sound-effects wizard Jimmy MacDonald; now it's Wayne Allwine.

During World War II Mickey had this body part tucked inside his pants for a change.

Of ten, twenty, or thirty years, length of his "retirement" between *The Simple Things* and *Mickey's Christmas Carol.*

Mickey has been seen wearing a watch with this Disney executive's picture on it.

DR. SEUSS

The good-hearted elephant who heard a "Who" and hatched an egg.

"And to think that I saw it on Mulberry Street," which was rejected twenty-eight times.

Famous for his five hundred hats, he saved a kingdom from gooey, green, destructive oobleck.

Dr. Seuss created this Oscar-winning cartoon character who made sounds like "boing."

When Dr. Seuss got an honorary degree, the audience quoted from this book about Sam-I-Am.

THE FLINTSTONES

Town the Flintstones call home.

Chip off the old Flintstone with her own cereal.

It's where Fred took the family in the opening of every show.

The Flintstones celebrated this anniversary October 14, 1985.

Fred and Barney were lodge members of this "Loyal Order."

THE JETSONS	BATMAN	POPEYE

The Jetsons' maid, Rosie, and George's office supervisor, Uniblab, are these.

In DC Comics today, Batman and this "Man of Steel" are no longer portrayed as friends.

She has a swan neck, a pickle nose, and measurements of 19–19–19.

Member of the family who attends the Little Dipper School.

The Batman first appeared in issue no. 27 of this comic book, dated May 1939.

This friend of Popeye's was born in a hamburger joint in Ocean Park Pier, California.

While Spacely made sprockets, Cogswell made these.

Batman's on-again-off-again love interest, Selina Kyle, has this costumed identity.

Called Brutus in comic strips, Popeye's 372–pound archenemy has this name in films and on TV.

Best known as Blondie in films, she provides Jane Jetson with her voice.

In the 1960s TV series a sign outside the Batcave indicated this was fourteen miles away.

This name for an army vehicle may be from the yellow fourth-dimensional animal who eats orchids.

Before the Jetsons got him, he belonged to zillionaire J. P. Gottrockets and was named Tralfax.

In a 1949 time-travel tale, Batman and Robin pooled their efforts to save this thirteenth-century explorer.

One of Popeye's four nephews in the animated cartoons.

JEOPARDY!

MICKEY MOUSE	DR. SEUSS	THE FLINTSTONES
Who is Minnie?	Who is Horton?	What is Bedrock?
Who provides the voice for Mickey Mouse?	What was his first (published) (children's) book?	Who is Pebbles?
What is his tail?	Who is Bartholomew Cubbins?	What is the drive-in?
What is thirty years?	What is Gerald McBoing-Boing?	What is the twenty-fifth?
Who is Michael (D.) Eisner?	What is *Green Eggs and Ham?*	What is the "Loyal Order of Water Buffalos"?

THE JETSONS	BATMAN	POPEYE
What are robots?	Who is Superman?	Who is Olive Oyl?
Who is Elroy?	What is Detective Comics?	Who is (J. Wellington) Wimpy?
What are cogs?	Who is Catwoman?	What is Bluto?
Who is Penny Singleton?	What was Gotham City?	What is Jeep?
Who is Astro?	Who was Marco Polo?	Who is Peepeye, Pipeye, Poopeye, or Pupeye?

DOUBLE JEOPARDY

MARILYN MONROE

Marilyn claimed to be a direct descendant of this U.S. president.

In the fall of 1953, Marilyn made her TV debut on this "stingy" comedian's program.

In 1956 Marilyn converted to Judaism before she married this playwright.

At Marilyn's funeral, this director of the Actors Studio, with whom she once studied, gave the eulogy.

Marilyn sang a sexy rendition of "Heat Wave" in this 1954 movie musical.

DOLLY PARTON

While looking at a famous southern California sign, Dolly came up with this name for her amusement park.

Dolly was most embarrassed when she entered a Dolly Parton look-alike contest and didn't do this.

Piece of clothing Dolly's mother made for her that inspired one of her early hit songs.

In this movie, Miss Parton played Miss Mona.

In 1967 she sang on this country singer's TV show, and in 1968 they won CMA's best vocal group.

RITA HAYWORTH

Margarita Carmen Cansino.

In 1943, Rita announced her engagement to Victor Mature but married this actor-director instead.

Rita was discovered while doing this in a Tijuana nightclub when she was only thirteen.

Rita was such a bombshell that her pin-up picture from this magazine was pasted on an atom bomb.

Rita's agile leading man in two films, *You Were Never Lovelier* and *You'll Never Get Rich*.

BETTE MIDLER	CHER	BROOKE SHIELDS SAYS
Her heavenly nickname.	As "Bonnie Jo Mason," Cher recorded a love song with this Fab Four drummer.	If you have trouble doing this at night, Brooke suggests wearing a mask or listening to harp music.
A View from a Broad and *The Saga of Baby Divine.*	Cher's second husband and father of Elijah Blue was this rock singer.	Brooke chills two spoons in ice water and holds them against these body parts when they look puffy.
In her first all-comedy album, this "Will Be Flung Tonight."	Shortly after guest hosting Merv Griffin's show in 1971, Sonny and Cher got their own show on this network.	She warns that this habit can turn your teeth brown and make your clothes closet stink.
This ill-fated 1982 movie, in which she played a casino singer, lived up to its name and sent her into therapy.	Besides Armenian, Turkish, and French ancestry, Cher is also partly descended from these Indians.	According to Brooke, girls should always put this on their earlobes, as well as their faces.
In a 1985 poll, she topped Sally Field and Olivia Newton-John as least likely to succeed in this.	In 1985 she was named "Woman of the Year" by this organization at Harvard.	Brooke massages a little baby oil into these instead of applying a base coat.

DOUBLE JEOPARDY!

MARILYN MONROE

Who was James Monroe?

Who was Jack Benny?

Who is Arthur Miller?

Who was Lee Strasberg?

What is *There's No Business Like Show Business?*

DOLLY PARTON

What is Dollywood?

What is win?

What is a coat ("Coat of Many Colors")?

What is *The Best Little Whorehouse in Texas*?

Who is Porter Wagoner?

RITA HAYWORTH

What was Rita Hayworth's real name?

Who was Orson Welles?

What was dancing?

What was *Life?*

Who was Fred Astaire?

BETTE MIDLER	CHER	BROOKE SHIELDS SAYS
What is "The Divine Miss M"?	Who is Ringo Starr?	What is sleeping?
What are her books?	Who is Greg Allman?	What are her eyes?
What is "Mud"?	What is CBS?	What is smoking?
What is *Jinxed?*	What is Cherokee?	What is foundation? (ACC: makeup)
What is marriage?	What is the Hasty Pudding Club?	What are her (finger) nails?

FINAL JEOPARDY!

**CATEGORY:
LEADING LADIES**

The two blonde sex symbols who made their last completed films with Clark Gable, one released in 1931, one in 1961.

FINAL JEOPARDY!

Who were Jean Harlow and Marilyn Monroe? (The films were *Saratoga* and *The Misfits*.)

Words to the Wise:
Contestant Briefing Notes

When contestants are selected to appear on the show, they arrive at our studios at 10:30 A.M. on either a Sunday or a Monday, and from the moment they set foot on the lot they are accompanied everywhere by our contestant coordinators. First, there is a briefing about procedures, rules, and strategy. Here's what you'd hear if you were at the studio:

> Welcome to what we hope will be a fun, perhaps even profitable, day for you. Having been selected to appear on the program, you should count yourself as a winner because, of the hundreds of thousands who try out, few are chosen.
>
> Now, some comments about security. You are not to speak to anyone during your visit, other than the contestant coordinators, a representative of the ABC network (here to monitor security and fairness procedures), and Alex Trebek. No one is to wander. Do not go anywhere without a contestant coordinator. Violation of the these procedures can lead to immediate ineligibility.
>
> During the taping, no swearing. Enthusiasm is welcomed, tantrums are not. If you feel something happened during the game that is unfair (e.g., you didn't get credit for an answer you thought was right), the time to point this out is during a commercial break, when contestant coordinators approach the podiums. We are onstage with

the contestants at every break, and we'll be happy to check out any discrepancies.

RULES OF THE GAME

At the start of the game our returning champion picks the category and dollar amount. Alex reads the clue.

When he finishes the clue, a light surrounding the game board comes on. When that happens, you can ring in. *You must wait for the light.* If you ring in too soon, you will lock yourself out for two tenths of a second. If locked out, watch the red light on your lectern, and when it goes out, if another contestant has not rung in yet, you can hit your button again.

Alex calls on the contestant who rings in first, and a white light on his or her podium will light up. You'll have five seconds to answer. If your response is correct, money will be added to your total; if it's incorrect, money is deducted. If the first contestant is incorrect, Alex will say so, and the light around the game board will again come on, and the two remaining contestants can ring in. The procedure continues if the second contestant is incorrect.

You cannot ring in again on the same question if you have answered incorrectly, or time has run out.

ROUND 1: JEOPARDY!

Dollar amounts are one hundred to five hundred, and there is one Daily Double on the board. If you land on it, you can bet up to five hundred dollars even if you don't have that much in your total. If you have more than five hundred dollars, you can bet any part of your total.

Important: Watch your categories and listen carefully to the clues, as they often are worded in a fashion that leads to the correct response.

If you are having difficulty ringing in, we will come up during all commercial breaks and try to find out what you are doing wrong. For instance, if you keep the button permanently depressed, you will simply be locking yourself out.

ROUND 2: DOUBLE JEOPARDY!

This is played the same as round one, but the dollar amounts are two hundred to one thousand, and there are two Daily Doubles on the board. If you land on the Daily Double, you can bet up to one thousand dollars, if your total is less than that. If your total is more, you can wager any or all of that amount.

This round goes straight through without commercial interruption, and you should play aggressively, moving the game along so that all the windows are revealed, allowing you the maximum opportunity to build up your total.

FINAL JEOPARDY!

Only players with positive money totals play Final Jeopardy! Even if you have only a few hundred dollars and your two opponents are far ahead, don't despair; you still have a chance, since they have to bet against each other.

There is a two-minute commercial break prior to Final Jeopardy! We will bring you a pencil and paper so that you can calculate your wager. If you need more than two minutes, we will stop taping to accommodate you.

Important: After you have written your wager on the electronic screen, you cannot change it, so be sure you have calculated carefully before writing. *And make certain your response is in the form of a question!*

You have thirty seconds during which to write your response to Final Jeopardy! and at the end of that time your electronic pen will stop writing. Get your answer down as quickly as possible. If you want to change your mind, just scratch out and write again. But *quickly.*

AFTERWARD

If you become a five-time champion, you will be invited back for the Tournament of Champions.

Cash and prizes are not distributed until your program airs.

If anyone from the press approaches you for an interview, please do not reveal the outcome of your appearance until the program airs.

FINALLY

Jeopardy! is a game. It is meant to be fun, and being here should be a special day for you, whatever the outcome. You are all very bright people, so winning usually comes down to your familiarity with the categories that pop up in your particular game. If the categories are good ones for you, your score will reflect this. If you are not crazy about the categories, just play the game—you might find that you know more than you think you do. Believe me, anything can happen, so never be discouraged.

When you are introduced on the show and you walk to your podium, look straight ahead and smile. You'll be glad you did when you watch the show yourself.

After this briefing, the contestants then have the opportunity to play a mock game in the studio, try out the buzzers, and get the feel of it all. Then it's time for makeup and *Jeopardy!*

During the tapings, contestants awaiting their turn are allowed to watch from the audience. However, during the tournaments, contestants are completely isolated from the studio until it is their time to compete. Why? Because to qualify for the semifinals of the tournament, contestants must either win or be one of four highest-scoring second-place finishers. If contestants know the dollar totals of players taping prior to them, they could play only to beat those totals, rather than going for the win, and this would give them an unfair advantage.

Movie Madness

JEOPARDY!

CIRCUS MOVIES	PIRATE MOVIES	SCREEN GEMS
In the classic Disney film, Dumbo's ability to do this makes him a circus sensation.	In this 1935 film that made him a star, Errol Flynn was Dr. Peter Blood, a physician who turns to piracy.	In this 1971 James Bond film, the evil Blofeld was a diamond smuggler.
Betty Hutton performed many of her own aerial stunts in this 1952 circus epic.	Anthony Quinn was a pirate stuck with stowaway children in the film *A High Wind in* this place.	The title of this 1969 Hitchcock film refers to the code name of a ring of spies.
He played circus owner Larson E. Whipsnade in *You Can't Cheat an Honest Man.*	Silent screen swash-buckler whose film *The Black Pirate* has been called a "definitive pirate movie."	It was the sequel to *Romancing the Stone.*
The elephant stole the show in this Doris Day musical based on Billy Rose's stage spectacular.	Robert Newton played this pirate before Peter Ustinov played his ghost in a Disney film.	This 1948 film based on a Steinbeck story about a fisherman was shot in Mexico.
This former circus acrobat got to play a circus acrobat in the 1956 film *Trapeze.*	Ingrid Bergman's husband in *Casablanca,* he played a pirate captain in *Pirates of Tripoli.*	In this film, when Cary Grant told Grace Kelly her necklace was imitation, she answered, "I'm not."

MOVIE ARTISTS

Charles Laughton traveled to Holland to research his role as this great Dutch artist.

The 1956 film in which Kirk Douglas cut off his ear.

Lucky Tony Franciosa got to paint Ava Gardner when he played this role in *The Naked Maja.*

Gene Kelly played an ex-GI struggling as an artist in Montmartre in this classic 1951 musical.

In a hauntingly romantic film, Joseph Cotten paints a portrait of this girl and then falls in love with her.

MOVIE AUTHORS

Sixteen years before he went wild in *Network,* he played Wilde in *The Trials of Oscar Wilde.*

Persian poet portrayed by Cornel Wilde in a 1957 film; watch it with "a jug of wine" and "a loaf of bread."

Turhan Bey, as this "fabled" author, spent *A Night in Paradise* with Merle Oberon but without a "moral."

In *Devotion,* Nancy Coleman, Olivia De Havilland, and Ida Lupino played these devoted British siblings.

Though he never won a Nobel Prize, *The Life of* this Frenchman won a 1937 Best Picture Oscar.

MORE MOVIE AUTHORS

Herbert Marshall played him in *The Moon and Sixpence* and *The Razor's Edge.*

As this author of *The Man Who Would be King,* Christopher Plummer listened to Michael Caine tell the film's story.

Beloved Infidel was Sheilah Graham's 1959 version of her affair with this novelist.

Oscar-winner who played Robert Browning in 1934 and Mark Twain ten years later.

Richard Chamberlain limped through this romantic lead in *Lady Caroline Lamb.*

JEOPARDY!

CIRCUS MOVIES	PIRATE MOVIES	SCREEN GEMS
What is fly?	What is *Captain Blood?*	What is *Diamonds Are Forever?*
What is *The Greatest Show on Earth?*	What is Jamaica?	What is *Topaz?*
Who was W. C. Fields?	Who was Douglas Fairbanks (Senior)?	What is *The Jewel of the Nile?*
What is *Jumbo?* (ACC: *Billy Rose's Jumbo*)	Who was Blackbeard?	What is *The Pearl?*
Who is Burt Lancaster?	Who is Paul Henried?	What is *To Catch a Thief?*

MOVIE ARTISTS	MOVIE AUTHORS	MORE MOVIE AUTHORS
Who was Rembrandt (Van Rijn)?	Who was Peter Finch?	Who is Somerset Maugham?
What is *Lust for Life?*	Who is Omar Khayyam?	Who is Rudyard Kipling?
Who was (Francisco) Goya?	Who is Aesop?	Who is F. Scott Fitzgerald?
What is *An American in Paris?*	Who are the Brontë sisters?	Who is Fredric March?
Who was Jennie (Appleton)? (ACC: Jennifer Jones)	Who was Emile Zola?	Who is Lord Byron?

DOUBLE JEOPARDY!

HOLLYWOOD QUEENS

Von Stroheim directed this star in *Queen Kelly,* but she bossed him around in *Sunset Boulevard.*

When Gable was named king of the movies, this *Thin Man* star was voted queen.

This sheep queen of *The Thorn Birds* was *Cattle Queen of Montana* in the 1954 film.

This Oscar winner had had four husbands by the time she starred in *The Virgin Queen.*

Off-screen, she was once "queen" of Hilton Hotels; on-screen, she was *Queen of Outer Space.*

MOVIE ROYALTY

The evil queen in *Snow White* was obsessed with the beauty opinions of this household object.

He was Philip II of Spain in *Fire over England* but was more famous for playing Lincoln.

The French or the Egyptian actor cast as Austrian Crown Prince Rudolf in 1936 and 1968 versions of *Mayerling.*

Robert Morley tried to have his cake and eat it, too, as this king in *Marie Antoinette.*

Dressed in men's clothes, Garbo played not a drag queen but this Swedish queen.

BACK TO THE BEACH

Lori Loughlin said this star who played her mother "looked more like my mom than my real one."

His character's never called by name during the film, only "The Big Kahuna" or "Honey" or "Dear."

In 1987, Bob Denver not only reprised this role in *Back to the Beach* but on *Alf* and *The New Gidget,* too.

He had another "big adventure" singing "Surfin' Bird" in the film.

Among the people putting in cameo appearances are the people who played this family from Mayfield.

HOLLYWOOD FRUITS

Jimmy Cagney was going to shove an omelette in Mae Clarke's face, but this fruit was less of a mess.

Humphrey Bogart went bananas when these disappeared in *The Caine Mutiny*.

He became Joe E. Brown's fiancée in *Some Like It Hot*.

Sidney Poitier film whose fruity title came from Langston Hughes's *Montage of a Dream Deferred*.

Name of the Devil as played by future Martian Ray Walston on Broadway and onscreen in *Damn Yankees*.

MOVIE MUSICALS

He directed *Finian's Rainbow*, but he's better known for *The Godfather*.

The two ex-Beatles who played themselves in *Give My Regards to Broad Street*.

This innovative film ended with a complete ballet danced to Gershwin music by Gene Kelly and Leslie Caron.

Bob Hope called this Clint Eastwood's "most violent" film: "When Clint sings, that's violence."

She recreated her Broadway role in *Bells Are Ringing*, her last film before her untimely death.

MOVIE TITLE ROLES

Bullitt.

Barbarella.

Barbarosa.

The Barefoot Contessa.

Boxcar Bertha.

DOUBLE JEOPARDY!

HOLLYWOOD QUEENS	MOVIE ROYALTY	BACK TO THE BEACH
Who is Gloria Swanson?	What is her mirror?	Who is Annette Funicello?
Who is Myrna Loy?	Who is Raymond Massey?	Who is Frankie Avalon?
Who is Barbara Stanwyck?	Who is Charles Boyer or Omar Sharif?	Who is Gilligan?
Who is Bette Davis?	Who is Louis XVI?	Who is Pee Wee Herman?
Who is Zsa Zsa Gabor?	Who is Queen Christina?	Who are the Cleavers?

HOLLYWOOD FRUITS	MOVIE MUSICALS	MOVIE TITLE ROLES
What is a grapefruit?	Who is Francis Coppola?	Who did Steve McQueen play?
What are strawberries?	Who are Paul McCartney and Ringo Starr?	Who did Jane Fonda play?
Who is Jack Lemmon?	What was *An American in Paris?*	Who did Willie Nelson play?
What is *A Raisin in the Sun?*	What was *Paint Your Wagon?*	Who did Ava Gardner play?
What is Applegate?	Who was Judy Holliday?	Who did Barbara Hershey play?

FINAL JEOPARDY!

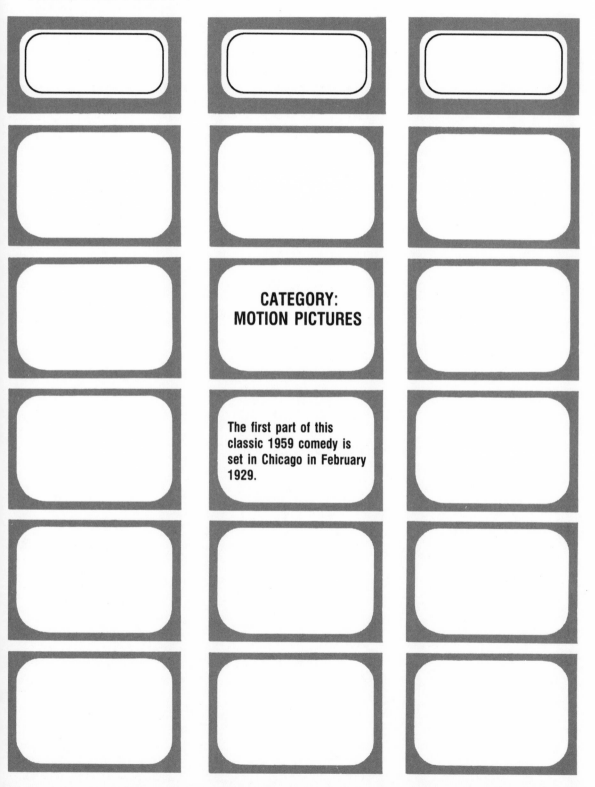

**CATEGORY:
MOTION PICTURES**

The first part of this classic 1959 comedy is set in Chicago in February 1929.

FINAL JEOPARDY!

What is *Some Like It Hot?*

An Interview with Art Fleming

Peter Barsocchini: Do people still recognize you from the show?

Art Fleming: All the time. I never get tired of it. I think the show was the high point of my life.

PB: When you were first approached about *Jeopardy!* you had never done a game show, right?

AF: Everything but. I had been on the Broadway stage when I was four years old, and I've done about everything you can do in show business—radio, television, motion pictures, even carnivals and circuses. I was the front man at carnivals: "Tell ya' what I'm gonna do, got a little show for you!" That kind of thing. So when Merv presented the idea of a game show, I figured this was something I'd never done before. I had lunch with Merv and Julann and they presented the idea. I happen to have a kooky mind that remembers little-known facts, so this show sounded fun. I thought it might run three months, six months, who knows? I decided to give it a shot. Twelve and a half years later, 2,858 shows, and we realized we were the beginning of the trivia craze. And it changed my life, because I've done forty-eight motion pictures, three television series, thousands of guest appearances, but everyone remembers me for *Jeopardy!*

PB: Did you ever miss a taping?

AF: Never, not one. Did them all.

PB: When the show started, did you think it might be too difficult for the contestants?

AF: Oddly, the toughest thing for the contestants was that for your entire life you're told that if you want to know something, ask a question. Now, here comes a show that gives you the answer and wants you to come up with the appropriate question. This discombobulates your thinking. It took me a couple of weeks to think in this backward fashion—answer, then question. And it has become a pattern in people's minds. To this day, I watch contestants on other game shows giving their answers in the form of a question. And the hosts have to remind them they are not on *Jeopardy!*

PB: What did it take to be a good *Jeopardy!* contestant?

AF: You had to have a smattering of knowledge, a broad base. And we didn't want college professors who were all brains and no personality, nor did we want the hip character with all personality and no knowledge. So it took people who had a little knowledge about a lot of things, and at the same time had the attitude that they were there to have fun, who realized it was a game, after all. Good players came in with the attitude that if they got the first few questions right, they were playing with house money, so they gambled with it.

PB: Any contestant you remember in particular?

AF: There was a fellow who was a radar man on a submarine. He had only two years of high school, but in the sub he had plenty of time to read everything, from books to cigar-band labels. He won everything, including the Tournament of Champions. What a great player he was.

PB: Did contestants give you a variety of reasons for wanting to be on the show?

AF: For a great many of them, they had something to prove. Remember, this was the sixties, so we had a lot of housewives, and they wanted to prove that just because they were home all day didn't mean they were lacking smarts. We'd get cab drivers and the like, and they felt they knew just as much as anybody else. Often more. And for most, it wasn't the money. I still get letters from people who were on the show and they say "I only won four hundred dollars but I had a great time." I'm sure it's still that way.

PB: Did any of the contestants ever take issue with you, sure they were right when you ruled them wrong?

AF: Very rarely. The staff checked and cross-checked the material quite carefully, with viable, well-known sources. But I remember one woman who took issue. The correct question in the biblical category was "What is Jericho?" And she said, "Damascus" and I ruled her wrong. Well, she came up with ten sources confirming her answers, and we had ten sources confirming ours. So we brought her back for another show, and she won a lot more money.

PB: What kind of preparation would you do for the show?

AF: I would see the game only fifteen minutes before we taped the show. And it was a matter of making certain I knew the information and understood the abbreviations. If I saw the phrase *comm,* it could have been *commissar, committee, communist, commission,* so in my mind I had to have a picture of the slot that answer was in and be clear on the meaning. The show was even faster in the early days than it is now, so concentration was the key.

PB: Did you have favorite categories?

AF: Yes, and still do, since I watch the show often: History, Music, Motion Pictures, Literature, Sports. Those were categories I liked, so that was the information I retained. I didn't care for Mythology. People say, "Gee, Art, you must be a genius playing *Jeopardy!* after all those years," but, like the audience, I tuned out the information I really wasn't interested in. But I remember the stuff from my favorite categories.

PB: Did you see a particular strategy that worked for the best players, week in and week out?

AF: If you hoarded the money—remember in those days, the contestants kept what they earned, even if they lost—you lost. The gamblers did pretty well. If they had five hundred bucks and hit the Daily Double, they would bet three hundred of it. Those were the people who won on the show.

PB: The show had totally different technology in your day, humans running the game board instead of computers . . .

AF: Stagehands using hand-lettered answers. They had to pull the cards as I read the answer. And that lent itself to error. Sometimes the cards got stuck, or came in upside down, and I'd have to ad lib, "Well, guys are backstage with a keg of beer and having a good time." We always had fun with the mistakes.

PB: What did you enjoy most about hosting the show?

AF: The mental exercise. You'd get a big kick out of having a tidbit of information that your friends didn't have. It's fun to know things, that's why trivia is so popular today. You tell friends something they don't know and they're impressed. And the kind of information we had was quick snippets of knowledge, nothing long or drawn-out. It's just good mental fun. And when you're in a bar with the guys having a drink, it comes in handy.

PB: Do people expect you to settle trivia disputes?

AF: All the time. I'll be having dinner in a restaurant and people will approach me and say, "My wife and I were arguing about so-and-so, and we knew you'd have the answer." Luckily, I usually do.

I was a guest on *Hollywood Squares* as the "secret square." I was worth $11,100. And the host, Peter Marshall, said, "In 1938, which of these three women won the Wimbledon tennis title?" And he gave the list. I don't know a thing about tennis, but I took my best guess, making it look like I was certain. You were told to fake it if you didn't know. So I said so-and-so, no doubt about it. And Peter Marshall looks at me with great doubt, and turns to the woman contestant and says, "Is Art right or wrong?" And she looks at me with big eyes and her heart wide open and says, "Art Fleming wouldn't lie. He's right." Thank God I guessed right.

PB: What about celebrity contestants?

AF: We had them, and they would play for charity. They took it seriously. Rod Serling, for example, loved the game, and you know that he was a very bright man. His first answer was "Westernmost capitol on the Iberian peninsula." And he replied, "What is Portugal?" I told him we needed more specific information. And he said, "What is Argentina?" And as soon as he said that he stopped, stunned, and said, "I don't believe I said Argentina is the capital of Portugal." It shattered him, because he knew it was Lisbon but the word didn't come out of his mouth. From that moment on he couldn't remember a thing on the show. The wildest celebrity we had was Mel Brooks. He came on our two thousandth show, doing his character of the Two Thousand Year Old Man. I asked him if two thousand years ago he had played *Jeopardy!* His character responded with, "When we left the cave, we were always in jeopardy!"

Phylis Newman was maybe the best celebrity contestant. When she played, she gave it her all, no fooling around. And Robert Klein was very good, and of course he still does comedy about me and *Jeopardy!*

PB: What about your life today?

AF: Busier than ever. Living in St. Louis. I do a two-hour radio talk show every day and a trivia show Sunday nights. And I do quite a few lectures every year, speaking on motivation and enthusiasm. And everywhere I go, they want to hear about *Jeopardy!*

Teen Tournament

JEOPARDY!

FOUR-LETTER WORDS

One of these was home to a nursery-rhyme old woman with "so many children."

Sport in which you hit a ball with a club; in fact, its name backward means "to beat harshly."

Meaning merge, this word was created by merging melt and weld.

Slew is the past tense of this word.

It can precede *horse, continent* or *side of the moon.*

FEBRUARY

Exact date of the next leap year.

On February 3 this country celebrates the Festival of Setsubun to drive away evil spirits.

Chicago mayor Anton Cermak was killed in 1933 when Giuseppe Zangara fired at this president-elect.

On Feb. 1, 1790, the Supreme Court met for the first time, and this chief justice presided.

Two great astronomers born in February—one in Poland in 1473 and one in Italy in 1564.

COOKING

This part of an egg is one of the best thickeners for soup.

Joy of Cooking says when baking white bread you should do this to your flour before you measure it.

As its name indicates, this pulled candy was originally made with H_2O from the ocean.

The Bermuda and sweet Spanish varieties of these are so mild they can be used raw in salads.

This meat is traditionally served with mint sauce or mint jelly.

RADIO AND TV	HEADS OF GOVERNMENT	HEAVY METAL
During a fight between Roy Innis and some skinheads, this talk show host got his nose broken.	Chancellor Helmut Kohl.	Name two types of current and you'll have the name of this currently popular metal group.
Famed radio deejay Robert Weston Smith is better known by this name—O-W-W-W!	President Hosni Mubarak.	In 1987 this group's fans experienced "hysteria" over their follow-up album to "Pyromania."
Whether airing on Showtime or the Fox network, It's this comedian's *Show.*	State President F. W. DeKlerk.	Jessica Hahn plays the "Wild Thing" in this comedian's video that featured many metal stars.
Now in its eighth year, this national radio show that Bob Coburn hosts lets you call in and talk to rock stars.	President Carlos Salinas de Gortari.	Parents might want an antidote to this group's hit album *Look What the Cat Dragged In.*
Believe it or not, this TV show spoofing superheroes had a theme song called "Believe It or Not."	King Fahd.	One of the two "colorful" groups with whom David Coverdale has been lead singer.

JEOPARDY!

FOUR-LETTER WORDS	FEBRUARY	COOKING
What is *shoe?*	What is (Saturday) February 29, 1992?	What is the yolk?
What is *golf?*	What is Japan?	What is sift it?
What is *meld?*	Who was FDR?	What is saltwater taffy?
What is *slay?*	Who was John Jay?	What are onions?
What is *dark?*	Who are (Nicolaus) Copernicus and Galileo (Galilei)?	What is lamb?

RADIO AND TV	HEADS OF GOVERNMENT	HEAVY METAL
Who is Geraldo Rivera?	What is West Germany?	What is AC/DC?
Who is Wolfman Jack?	What is Egypt?	What is Def Leppard?
Who is Garry Shandling?	What is South Africa?	Who is Sam Kinison?
What is *Rockline?*	What is Mexico?	What is Poison?
What was *The Greatest American Hero?*	What is Saudi Arabia?	What is Deep Purple or Whitesnake?

DOUBLE JEOPARDY!

FAMOUS TEENAGERS

This youthful outlaw's real name may have been Henry McCarty, and we're not kidding.

Teenage actress Tina Yothers plays typical teenager Jennifer Keaton on this sitcom.

Andre Agassi is one of this sport's new stars.

In 1560 this eighteen-year-old queen of Scotland was already a widow.

The last teenager to rule England.

JEWELRY

In the nursery rhyme, the lady at Banbury Cross has these on her fingers and bells on her toes.

New jewelry made of this tusk material is a pale cream color, but age may turn it yellow.

This type of engraved gem features a raised design, often a scene from classical mythology.

Handy Tan suntan lotion comes inside this piece of jewelry, so you can wear it to the beach.

A popular brand of jewelry sold in department stores, or the last name of a French impressionist.

ENGLISH LITERATURE

Polynesia the parrot taught him the language of birds.

The story of Little Dorrit's father in debtor's prison was based on his father's experiences.

Title character of H. G. Wells' 1897 novel who was heard more than seen.

Keeping the same initials, these sisters published under the pen names Currer, Ellis, and Acton Bell.

He wrote *The Lord of the Isles* five years after *The Lady of the Lake*.

ZOOLOGY

The desert-dwelling sand grouse uses its feathers to carry this back to its young.

This large animal's name comes from the Greek for "river horse" although it's more closely related to the pig.

One species of fish in Oman can regrow the optic lobes on this organ, the only vertebrate known to do so.

Pit organs in some snakes allow them to locate and strike at prey by sensing this.

This zoologist's writings include *My Friends, the Wild Chimpanzees* and *In the Shadow of Man.*

BODIES OF WATER

According to the Bible, John the Baptist baptized Jesus in the waters of this river.

This river forms more than half the border between Mexico and the United States.

Toronto, Canada, is on the shores of this Great Lake.

Almost completely surrounded by land, the name of this sea means "in the middle of land."

Famous in music, it flows nearly two thousand miles, from the Black Forest to the Black Sea.

HEAVY METALS

One of the three common metallic elements that is easily magnetized when put in a magnetic field.

Only gold and silver are more ductile than this metal, which is more valuable than either of them.

Soft solder is made of tin and this heavy metal that's so soft a fingernail can scratch it.

Its chemical symbol is Hg, from hydrargyrum, meaning "water silver."

The name of the stomach medicine Pepto-Bismol comes from the fact that it contains this heavy metallic element.

DOUBLE JEOPARDY!

FAMOUS TEENAGERS	JEWELRY	ENGLISH LITERATURE
Who was Billy the Kid? (ACC: William H. Bonney or William Bonney, Jr., or M. H. McCarty)	What are rings?	Who is Dr. Doolittle?
What is *Family Ties?*	What is ivory?	Who was Charles Dickens?
What is tennis?	What is a cameo?	Who is the Invisible Man?
Who was Mary, Queen of Scots? (ACC: Mary Stuart)	What is a bracelet?	Who were Charlotte, Emily, and Anne Brontë? (ACC: Brontë sisters)
Who was Queen Victoria?	What is Monet?	Who was Sir Walter Scott?

ZOOLOGY	BODIES OF WATER	HEAVY METALS
What is water?	What is the Jordan?	What is iron, cobalt, or nickel?
What is the hippopotamus?	What is the Rio Grande?	What is platinum?
What is the brain?	What is Lake Ontario?	What is lead?
What is heat (given off by the prey)?	What is the Mediterranean?	What is mercury?
Who is Jane Goodall?	What is the Danube River?	What is bismuth?

FINAL JEOPARDY

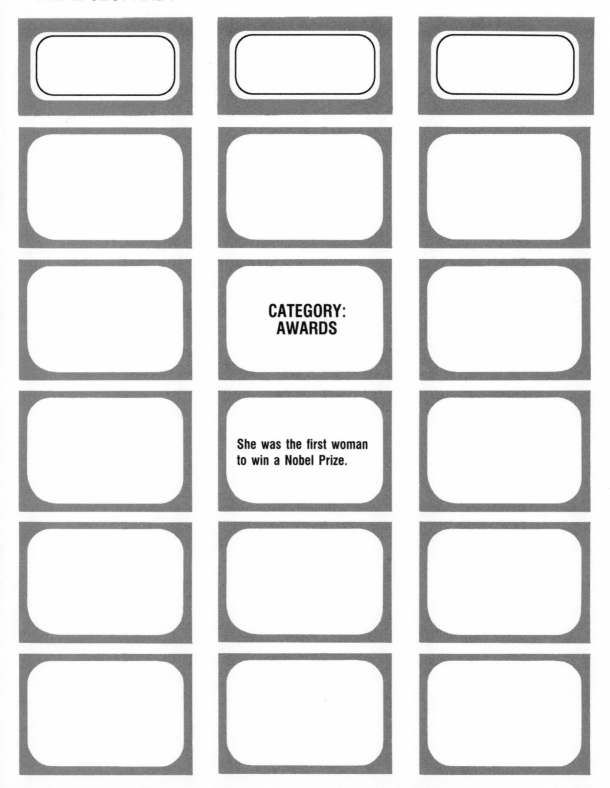

**CATEGORY:
AWARDS**

She was the first woman
to win a Nobel Prize.

FINAL JEOPARDY

Who is Marie Curie?

Tournament of Champions #2

JEOPARDY!

CORPORATE AMERICA	GARDENING	MYTHS AND LEGENDS
Joyce Hall began this Kansas City company selling postcards.	Dates and coconuts both grow on this type of tree.	A sincere cavalier, he fooled around with Guinevere.
G.E. was instrumental in starting this communications giant that it bought in 1986.	This relative of the onion is rarely grown from seed; it's grown from parts of its bulbs called cloves.	His ninth hurdle— Hippolyta's girdle.
This company's founder invented condensed milk.	Also known as plant lice, these garden pests secrete a "honeydew" that ants eat.	Through many a metaphysical joust he tried to win the soul of Faust.
Dole is the best-known brand name of this company founded by missionaries in Hawaii.	Azaleas are a member of this plant genus whose name means "rose tree."	A disembodied head or pumpkin was thrown at this poor country bumpkin.
This company that sells Kleenex and Huggies was founded in Neenah, Wisconsin, in 1872 and is still there.	Prairie sunset and sable are two of the bearded varieties of this spring flower.	While Ulysses was off fighting the war, she kept a lock on her bedroom door.

RECORD ALBUMS	SLAVERY	"CHAIN"'S

He's had the most top 40 and top 10 albums during the rock era—not bad for a man who's been singing since 1933.

In 1861 by imperial decree, Alexander II liberated forty million serfs in this country.

A shackled group of prisoners, they were formerly used to build roads in the southern United States.

"You Belong to the City" was part of this television show's number-one album.

This large Middle-Eastern country did not abolish slavery until 1962.

Knights wore this flexible armor of interlinked metal rings.

"Blue Bayou" and "It's So Easy" are both on her *Simple Dreams* album.

In 1865 this amendment to the Constitution abolished slavery in the United States.

In the U.S. Army it would be general to lieutenant general to major general to brigadier general.

This group's name was also the name of its first number-one album; the second was "Rumours."

The Compromise of 1850 banned the slave trade in Washington, D.C., and admitted this state as a free state.

The constellation Andromeda is sometimes given this nickname.

"Heart of Glass" was cut for this group's album *Parallel Lines.*

Eleven-letter word meaning the formal emancipation of a slave by his owner.

Completes the line from *The Communist Manifesto* "The proletarians . . ."

JEOPARDY!

CORPORATE AMERICA	GARDENING	MYTHS AND LEGENDS
What is Hallmark?	What is a palm tree?	Who was (Sir) Lancelot? (ACC: Launcelot)
What is RCA? (ACC: NBC)	What is garlic?	Who was Hercules?
Who is (Gail) Borden?	What are aphids?	Who is Mephistopheles? (ACC: The Devil, Satan)
What is Castle & Cooke?	What is *Rhododendron?*	Who is Ichabod Crane?
What is Kimberly-Clark?	What is an iris?	Who was Penelope?

RECORD ALBUMS	SLAVERY	"CHAIN"S
Who is Frank Sinatra?	What is Russia?	What is chain gang?
What was *Miami Vice?*	What is Saudi Arabia?	What is chain mail?
Who is Linda Ronstadt?	What is the Thirteenth Amendment?	What is the chain of command?
Who are Fleetwood Mac?	What is California?	What is the "Chained Lady"?
Who is Blondie?	What was manumission?	What is "have nothing to lose but their chains"?

DOUBLE JEOPARDY!

FAMOUS FIRSTS	LITERATURE	ARTISTS
The Anti-Masons were the first U.S. political party to hold one of these to choose its candidates.	He collaborated with ex-wife Margaret Bourke-White on documentaries but not on *God's Little Acre.*	He was one of the finest American portrait artists, but he's best remembered for his "code."
In 1874 cigar makers, not the ladies garment workers, became the first union to have this on their products.	His novels *Ragtime* and *World's Fair* were both set in New York City before World War II.	Jan Vermeer lived his entire life in this city known for its pottery.
In 1793 the first U.S. ship canal was built near Springfield in this state.	The title of this novel by Charles Jackson has become a catch phrase for a major drinking binge.	Sir Joshua Reynolds was knighted by this king in 1769.
A veteran of the last Mercury flight and Gemini 5, he was the first man to make two orbital flights.	Some of the stories and poems in *We Are Still Married* reflect on this author's life in Minnesota.	Norwegian whose painting *The Cry*, or *The Scream*, has been called "an icon of existential anguish."
The first woman to win a Pulitzer for fiction was this author of *The Age of Innocence*, in 1921.	We wonder what his grandfather, the adding machine inventor, would have thought of *Naked Lunch*.	Born in 1872, this Englishman known for black and white drawings was a leader of the art nouveau movement.

THE BODY HUMAN

These very fine blood vessels give oxygenated blood to the tissues and remove deoxygenated blood from them.

Rejection of organ transplants is caused by the reaction of this defense system.

Two of the three bones that meet at the shoulder.

Muscles used to move a limb away from the central line of the body.

A tricuspid insufficiency has nothing to do with the teeth but refers to a valve failure here.

PROVERBS

Every month *Reader's Digest* reminds us it's "the best medicine."

Samuel Johnson said, "When a man is tired of" this city, "he is tired of life."

Earlier than 400 B.C. Thucydides wrote that history tends to do this.

Jesus taught, "Greater love hath no man than" this.

"In the country of the blind," this man "is king."

TRAVEL AND TOURISM

The Rock has been called the grande dame of local hotels on this small peninsula.

The kind of currency you'd need to play the slot machines in the casino at Monte Carlo.

There are 137 of them in all, and they lead up from Rome's Piazza di Spagna.

African country in which you can visit Aberdare National Park and Mombasa Beach.

Brazilian airline whose name is an abbreviation of "Empresa de Viacao Aerea Rio Grandense."

DOUBLE JEOPARDY!

FAMOUS FIRSTS	LITERATURE	ARTISTS
What is a (nominating) convention?	Who was Erskine Caldwell?	Who was (Samuel F. B.) Morse? (ACC: Samuel Finley Breese Morse)
What is a union label?	Who is Edgar Lawrence (E. L.) Doctorow?	What is Delft?
What is Massachusetts?	What is *The Lost Weekend?*	Who was George III?
Who is Gordon Cooper?	Who is Garrison Keillor?	Who was (Edvard) Munch?
Who was Edith Wharton?	Who is William Burroughs?	Who was Aubrey Beardsley?

THE BODY HUMAN	PROVERBS	TRAVEL AND TOURISM
What are the capillaries?	What is laughter?	What is Gibraltar?
What is the immune system?	What is London?	What are francs?
What are the clavicle, the humerus, and the scapula?	What is "repeat itself"?	What are the Spanish Steps?
What are the abductor muscles? (ACC: abductors)	What is "that a man lay down his life for his friends"?	What is Kenya?
What is in the heart?	What is "the one-eyed man"?	What is Varig?

FINAL JEOPARDY!

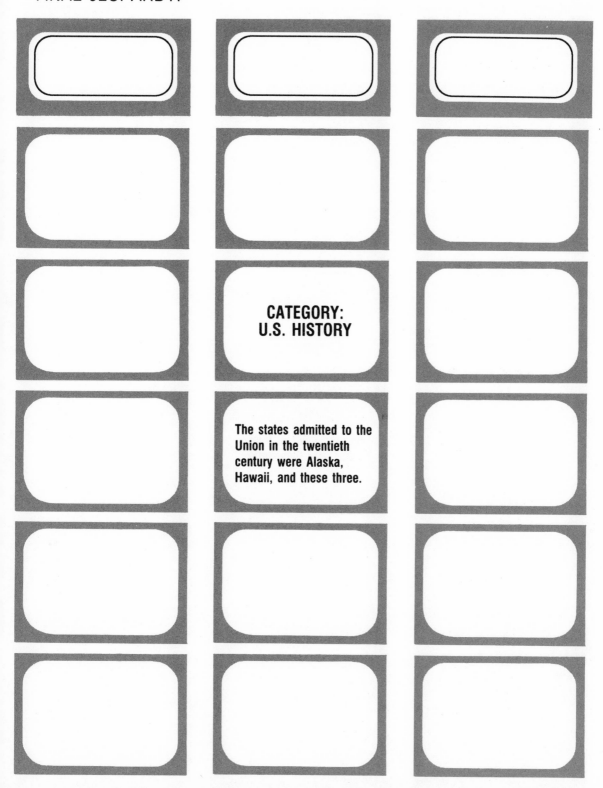

CATEGORY:
U.S. HISTORY

The states admitted to the Union in the twentieth century were Alaska, Hawaii, and these three.

FINAL JEOPARDY!

What are Arizona, New Mexico, and Oklahoma?

Tournament of Champions #3

JEOPARDY!

HOLLYWOOD HISTORY	WORLD GEOGRAPHY	1981
The plot for this early talkie parallels the story of Al Jolson's own life.	This capital city lies on the broad and shallow plain formed by the Moskva River and its tributaries.	In December a Peruvian named Javier Perez de Cuellar was named to this post.
This "Jezebel" said she named the statue Oscar after her first husband, Harmon Oscar Nelson, Jr.	You must remember this is the most populous city in Morocco, but Rabat is the capital.	Fifty-two people leaving this country January 20, 1981, made world headlines.
This 1976 film was based on F. Scott Fitzgerald's unfinished novel inspired by Irving Thalberg.	With less than 10 percent of the world's population, this continent creates more than one-third of its manufactures.	He became president of Egypt after the assassination of Anwar Sadat.
President of the MPPDA from 1922–45, he initiated a moral blacklist and was an author of the Production Code.	The Red Sea is considered an arm of this ocean.	He introduced his stainless-steel gull-winged sports car.
Creator of Andy Panda, he held the longest contract in Hollywood—fifty-eight years with Universal.	There used to be two countries with this name; now there's only one and its capital is Brazzaville.	Two of the three standard rates in effect during the year for a U.S. first-class letter.

WEATHER

For a storm to be called this, it must have winds greater than 32 mph and heavy snow.

Silver iodide or dry ice is used to do this to a cloud.

More tornadoes are recorded in the basin of this river than anywhere else in the world.

An old weather adage says "Red sky in the morning, sailors" do this.

Also called a vapor trail, it's a cloudlike streamer that forms behind jets at high altitudes.

THE WARS OF THE ROSES

Contrary to legend, a rose of this color may not have been a symbol of the House of Lancaster.

Skeletons found at this site may be those of the little princes who vanished during the wars.

Appropriate nickname of the Earl of Warwick, who was instrumental in making Edward IV rule.

Surprisingly, this king, who died at Bosworth Field, wasn't a bad-looking chap.

After the wars ended, Henry VII claimed the throne, founding this dynasty.

"NOTHING" DOING

What a magician says to the audience as he pushes up his shirt cuffs.

Little, unimportant things that you'd whisper in your beloved's ear.

Completes this line from *Macbeth:* "a tale told by an idiot, full of sound and fury . . ."

According to "Me and Bobby McGee," "Freedom's just another word for" this.

In 1856 Millard Fillmore was its candidate for president.

JEOPARDY!

HOLLYWOOD HISTORY	WORLD GEOGRAPHY	1981
What is *The Jazz Singer?*	What is Moscow?	What is secretary-general of the UN?
Who is Bette Davis?	What is Casablanca?	What is Iran?
What is *The Last Tycoon?*	What is North America?	Who is (Muhammed) Hosni Mubarak?
Who was Will Hays?	What is the Indian Ocean?	Who is John De Lorean?
Who is Walter Lantz?	What is the Congo?	What are 15¢, 18¢, and 20¢?

WEATHER	THE WARS OF THE ROSES	"NOTHING" DOING
What is a blizzard?	What is red?	What is "nothing up my sleeves"?
What is seed it? (ACC: make it rain)	What is the Tower of London?	What are "sweet nothings"?
What is the Mississippi?	What was "the kingmaker"?	What is "signifying nothing"?
What is "take warning"?	Who was Richard III?	What is "nothin' left to lose"?
What is a contrail?	What was the Tudor dynasty?	What is the Know-Nothing party?

DOUBLE JEOPARDY!

SCIENTISTS

He developed the V-2 for Germany and, while in Alabama, the Saturn V for the United States.

Published in 1897, *Work of the Digestive Glands* was the only book by this Russian physiologist.

The idea of horsepower originated with this Scottish engineer, the "father of the Industrial Revolution."

Dutch optician Hans Lippershey invented this scientific device in 1608.

For his invention of the electric battery, this Italian physicist was made a count in 1801.

THE CONSTITUTION

In May 1787 this Virginian was unanimously chosen president of the Constitutional Convention.

The convention was instructed by Congress to revise this existing document, not to write a new one.

Congress is authorized to "provide and maintain" this branch of the armed forces.

To be adopted, an amendment must be ratified by this fraction of the states.

The compromise that gave us a two-house Congress was proposed by this state, hence its nickname.

HISTORIC NAMES

This leader, not boxer Cassius Clay, founded the modern Egyptian kingdom in the 1800s.

In his youth, the ruthless Roman emperor Gaius Caesar was nicknamed this, meaning "little boot."

Pilgrim governor whose *History of Plimmoth Plantation* was first published 199 years after his death.

English king born on Christmas Eve 1167; he had no power or land as a youth and was nicknamed "Lackland."

In 1832 he said, "The bank, Mr. Van Buren, is trying to kill me, but I will kill it."

FRENCH LITERATURE	WISCONSINITES	FLOWERS AND TREES
In the 1840s Victor Hugo began writing this book using the title *Les Misères.*	Milwaukee native who met his British-born wife, Lynn Fontanne, in 1917 on Broadway.	While its name means flesh-colored, it's usually a white one that men wear on tuxedos.
Term for aesthetically elegant literature, it's French for "fine letters."	He was born in Grand Chute, Wisconsin, attended Marquette University, and was elected to the Senate in 1946.	Spruce, fir, and hemlock are part of this, the largest and best-known conifer family.
His most famous short stories include "Ball-of-Fat" and "The Necklace."	He was governor of Wisconsin and author of a series of books about a "bad boy."	It takes some four thousand purple autumn crocuses to get one ounce of this powder used as a yellow dye.
In 1677 this dramatist's play *Phèdre* was produced, and he became Louis XIV's official historian.	A native of Ripon, suffragist Carrie Chapman Catt founded this organization in 1920.	Varieties of this tree, noted for its wood, include the West Indian and Honduras.
This series by Balzac intertwines almost one hundred works and more than two thousand characters.	Elected governor of Wisconsin in 1900, this "Battling Bob" founded a dynasty of politicians and social reformers.	The bark of a tree surrounds the xylem, which is divided into the sapwood and this.

DOUBLE JEOPARDY!

SCIENTISTS	THE CONSTITUTION	HISTORIC NAMES
Who was Werner von Braun?	Who was George Washington?	Who was Muhammed Ali?
Who was Ivan Pavlov?	What were the Articles of Confederation?	What is Caligula?
Who was James Watt?	What is the navy?	Who was William Bradford?
What is the telescope?	What is three-fourths?	Who was King John?
Who was (Alessandro) Volta?	What is Connecticut?	Who was Andrew Jackson?

FRENCH LITERATURE	WISCONSINITES	FLOWERS AND TREES
What is *Les Miserables?*	Who is Alfred Lunt?	What is a carnation?
What is "belles-lettres"?	Who was Joseph McCarthy?	What is the pine family?
Who was Guy de Maupassant?	Who was (George W.) Peck?	What is saffron?
Who was Jean Racine?	What is the League of Women Voters?	What is mahogany?
What is *The Human Comedy?*	Who was (Robert) La Follette?	What is the heartwood?

FINAL JEOPARDY!

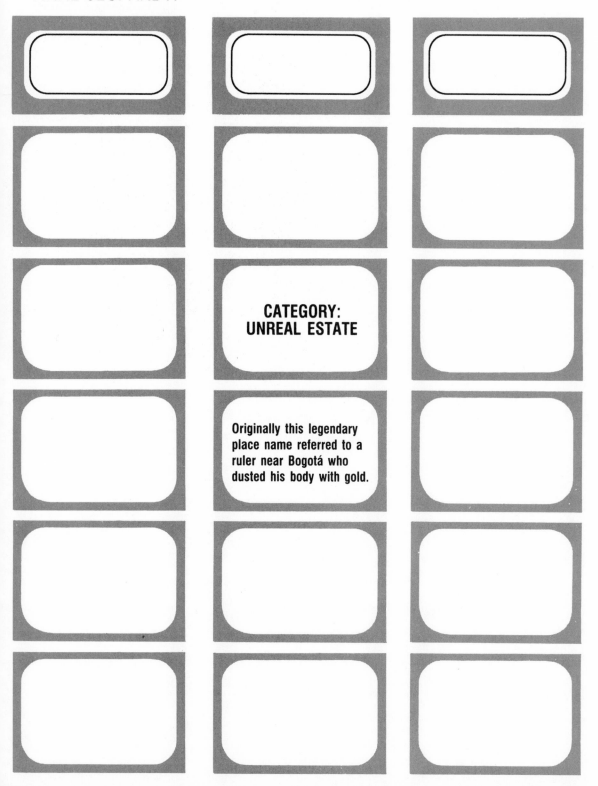

**CATEGORY:
UNREAL ESTATE**

Originally this legendary place name referred to a ruler near Bogotá who dusted his body with gold.

FINAL JEOPARDY!

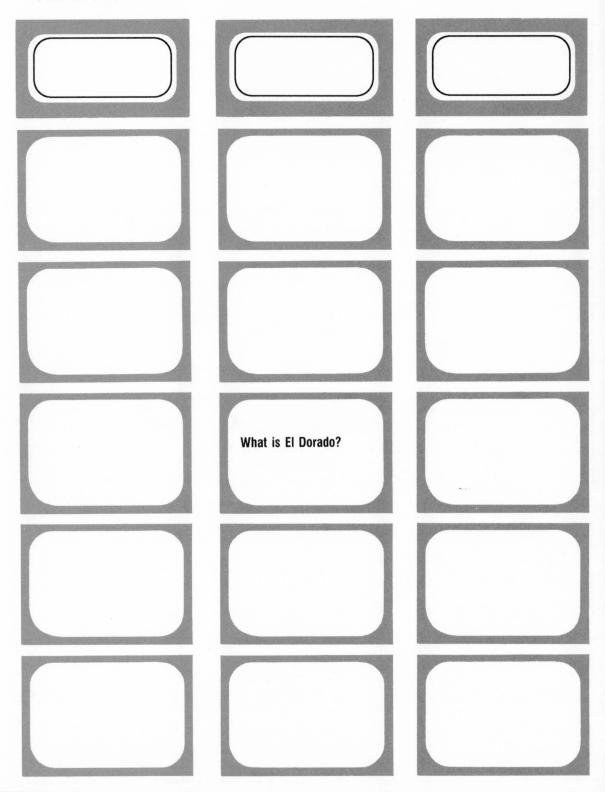

What is El Dorado?

- You've watched the show...
- You've read the book...
- Now...

PLAY PHONE JEOPARDY!

HOSTED BY ALEX TREBEK

Play **Phone Jeopardy!** on your touch tone phone and win at home today!

WIN CASH AND PRIZES!
CALL 1-900-436-8000

24 HOURS A DAY, 7 DAYS A WEEK